13.95/10.46

OFFICE ETIQUETTE AND PROTOCOL

by Grace Fox

LearningExpress • New York

Fox, Grace.
    Office etiquette and protocol/Grace Fox.
       p.   cm.—(Basics made easy)
    ISBN 1–57685–145–1
    1. Business etiquette.   I. Title.   II. Series.
HF5389.F69   1998
   395.5'2—dc21
                                        98–27451
                                          CIP

Printed in the United States of America
9 8 7 6 5 4 3 2 1
First Edition

For Further Information
For information on LearningExpress, other LearningExpress products, or bulk sales, please call or write to us at:
    LearningExpress®
    900 Broadway
    Suite 604
    New York, NY 10003
    212-995-2566

LearningExpress is an affiliated company of Random House, Inc.

ISBN 1–57685–145–1

7 85555 85145 0

CONTENTS

CHAPTER | 1

GETTING STARTED

You are about to start a new job—it may be your first or your fifth. Your excitement is dampened only by your fear. You want to do everything right, but how do you go about it?

A new job—or your first real foray into the working world—is always a scary experience. It is sometimes difficult to know what is expected of you in the workplace.

At the very least, you must know two things. Most people are aware of the first: You need to know how to do the job that you were hired to do. To this job, you bring a set of skills or a knowledge base that allows you to do that. Fewer people are aware of the other, equally important thing you must know to get along socially at work: office etiquette and protocol, that is, how to do the right thing in every work situation. Not knowing how to act in the workplace can hurt your chances for success every bit as much as not having the skills to do your job. In this book, you will learn everything you need to know about office etiquette and protocol.

To begin, you need to understand both etiquette and protocol. Etiquette, which involves social conventions and behavior, is mostly about treating others with kindness and graciousness. Knowing etiquette will give you a kind of polish that will make you highly promotable.

Protocol is a special branch of etiquette. Technically, it is the ceremonial forms that are used by diplomats and heads of state—making sure everyone is seated according to rank at a state dinner, for example. But protocol is also practiced in virtually every office as well. This isn't surprising when you think that most offices are organized in just as hierarchical a fashion as governments are.

The protocol practiced at work is less formal, and there are often no written guidelines, but this doesn't make it any less important or necessary. Knowing the informal, unwritten protocol of the workplace will make you a more savvy worker. When you understand office protocol, you will know, for example, where to seat the boss at a company luncheon you have organized, or whether you should call the Chairman of the Board by his first name.

Some office protocol is unique to a specific office; some is specific to a profession or a field of work; but much of it—most of it, in fact, as this book will reveal—is general to all offices and all fields. In other words, if you know how to behave in one workplace, you know how to behave in any of them.

If you follow the basic guidelines put forth in this book, you will develop an overall understanding of what office etiquette and protocol is all about. With this knowledge, it will only take another week or two for you to pick up on any rules that are specific to the office in which you work.

WHAT WILL YOU LEARN FROM THIS BOOK?

Office protocol is about how offices operate socially and, to a large extent, politically. For example, you will learn

- how to accept criticism graciously, and how to hand it out tactfully.
- how to get along with someone who considers you a rival.
- how to handle a boss, even if he or she is incompetent or difficult.

In this book, you will not learn how to hold a fork or whether to say "Excuse me" or "Pardon me" when apologizing to someone. These are rules of general etiquette, which you can find in another book. Instead of giving you the little details, *Office Etiquette and Protocol* will teach you about something far more useful: namely, how to get along at work in the general sense.

Why the Rules Matter

What's the point of learning a bunch of rules to use at work, you wonder? Aren't they just common sense? And specifically, what will they do for you?

If you follow accepted guidelines for behavior in the workplace, every aspect of work will go more smoothly. You and the people you work with will feel like part of a community—which an office is, after all. These guidelines also help to ensure that everyone will be treated the same, something that has not always happened in the office and doesn't necessarily happen in all offices today.

This book is important because much of office etiquette and protocol is unwritten. It is up to you to figure out what is expected of you rather than the other way around. You may be given an employee handbook, which may even cover some of the same subjects that are discussed in this book—dress codes, for example—but no office handbook will ever tell you the real inside story. You have to figure out how to dress to get promoted and whether you can put a magazine on your expense account when you travel on business.

Another very important reason to learn the correct etiquette and protocol for the workplace is that you, personally, will enjoy the benefits. Knowing your way around an office socially will advance your career by making you more successful and promotable.

How This Book Will Help You

This book is divided into 20 short chapters, each of which is devoted to a subject related to office etiquette and protocol. You should be able to read a chapter in less than half an hour. If you study one chapter a day, within a month, you'll know everything you need to know to be a successful, valued employee.

TEST YOUR OFFICE SAVVY

The following true-and-false quiz will test your awareness of office etiquette and protocol. Take it now and see how well you do. Then take it again after you have read this book—you'll be surprised at how much you have learned and how much more confident you are!

1. It's okay for me to show up late to work the first day of a new job because no one will have any real work for me to do anyway. True / False

2. I should wear casual clothes on Friday because all offices have "dress-down Fridays." True / False

3. I should call my new boss by his or her first name. True / False

4. It's cool to play some music on my voice mail instead of just leaving the same boring message as everyone else. True / False

5. A good way to put customers at ease is to use only my first name when I introduce myself. True / False

6. If someone I work with undermines my work to me personally, I should complain to my boss immediately. True / False

7. It's important to listen to all the office gossip so I can know what's going on. True / False

8. Coworkers who look older than me will be flattered when I address them as "Sir" and "Ma'am." True / False

9. If my boss invites me to a holiday dinner party at his or her house, then I should reciprocate by hosting dinner at my house. True / False

10. I can say anything I want to in office e-mail because it's illegal for other people to read it. True / False

11. I asked someone to supply a reference for me during my job hunt six months ago, so there's no need to ask again. References are good for one year. True / False

12. If a prospective employer asks me to send a résumé, I don't need to include a cover letter. True / False

13. During a job interview, one way to show I am an eager, assertive person is to bring up the subject of money. True / False

14. It sounds too formal to say anything but "Hello" when I answer my office telephone. True / False

15. Office affairs are taboo in most workplaces these days. True / False

Answers to the Quiz

1. **False.** Although there probably won't be any real work for you to do the first day on a new job, there will probably be some paperwork to fill out. At any rate, people are expecting you at a specific time. It is a serious mistake to show up even one minute late, because the first impression you will make is that you are lazy and lack initiative.

2. **False.** Not all offices practice dress-down Fridays, and even in those that do, figuring out exactly what constitutes "casual wear" can be a tricky business.

3. **False.** Call your boss Mr. or Ms. (Miss or Mrs.) So-and-So until he or she either suggests that you use his or her first name or, even though he or she doesn't mention it, you notice that everyone from the company president to the mail room clerk is on a first-name basis.

4. **False.** Leave the same outgoing voice message as everyone else. Save the "cool" one for your home answering machine.

5. **False.** If you use only your first name in an introduction, the customer might feel uncomfortable. It's also a youth-culture kind of thing to do among friends.

6. **False.** It's better to try to deal with this person on your own first. That way, if the comments continue and you later feel the need to approach your boss, you can report that you unsuccessfully tried to resolve the problem yourself.

7. **True and False.** Listen if you must, but let the rumors die with you. There is nothing wrong with hearing gossip—provided you know how to act a little uninterested—but it's never good to be the source of it.

8. **False.** Don't call anyone "Sir" or "Ma'am" in an office environment. Charming on certain social occasions, these titles can be off-putting in work situations.

9. **False.** If your boss has the entire department over for an annual event, you don't have to feel obligated to return the invitation—and doing so might be a little presumptuous.

10. **False.** Nothing is private about e-mail. It can be read by your secretary, your boss, the president of the company, the chairman of the board, and all your rivals.

11. **False.** Ask references whether you can use their names *every* time you begin a new round of job hunting.

12. **False.** Include a cover letter with every résumé, whether it's a formal "You don't know me, but ..." version or a handwritten note reminding the recipient that he or she requested a copy.

13. **False.** Job applicants as a rule do not bring up the subject of money, mostly because it doesn't come up until after you've been offered the job.

14. **False.** There are lots of options for how you can answer your phone at work. "Hello" is only one of them and is appropriate only under certain circumstances.

15. **True, but ...** Taboo or not, people meet, date, and marry fellow workers. The trick is to know how to conduct the coworker affair—and the marriage—so nobody feels uncomfortable.

And Remember ...

- On the job, your social skills count as much as your technical skills.
- Much of office etiquette and protocol consists of unwritten guidelines.
- Not knowing these guidelines can hold you back and keep you from being promoted.
- An office is a community: It functions best when everyone knows what is expected of him or her and what constitutes acceptable social behavior.

CHAPTER | 2

YOUR FIRST DAY OF WORK

Dressed to impress, you are as spiffed up as you can be! Your excitement and enthusiasm are catching. You certainly are ready to work. In fact, you feel pretty invaluable, because that is what you were told during the job interview. You walk through the door of your great new job—the one you hope will turn into a career—eager to turn your hand to whatever is asked of you.

And what, exactly, is asked of you? Nothing, really. No one pays much attention to you. Even your boss seems too busy to deal with you. Nobody gives you any real work, even though you're ready and raring to go. Has there been some kind of mistake? Did you show up at the wrong office? Did they have second thoughts about hiring you?

Chances are that yes, you are indeed in the right place, and no, there is no mistake. This scenario is pretty typical of a first day on a new job. Bosses ought to make time to usher in new employees, but something else usually intervenes, so the boss ends up paying more attention to the present than to you, the future of the business.

The first day on a new job can be a trying experience for a seasoned employee, let alone for someone who doesn't have a lot of work experience. You will have an easier time of it if you know what to expect, and what you can do to make the experience as pleasant as possible.

FIRST-DAY EXPECTATIONS

On the first day on any new job, you probably will

- arouse a certain degree of curiosity among your coworkers.
- meet and greet many people—some your superiors, some your inferiors, but think of all of them as your peers.
- begin to learn in a very general way the customs and protocol at your new workplace. (Start taking mental notes. This will help you later.)
- not do any "real" work. Unless the company is desperate for workers, most new employees are eased into their jobs slowly.

So, part of your assignment on the first day, and perhaps for as long as a week or more, is to manage to look busy while having nothing to do.

ALL EYES ARE ON YOU

Despite the apparent lack of interest in you, all eyes are on you from the minute you walk through the front door. You'll want to make a good impression. People are sizing you up as colleague, competitor, potential friend, and team player, so it behooves you to get off on the right foot.

Beat the Clock

The easiest way to impress everyone on your first day is to arrive on time. You may be the only person who shows up at this hour, even though you've been told that everyone starts at the same time.

If you notice that your new coworkers stroll in around 8:30 a.m., you may wonder why you bothered to get there at 8 a.m. sharp, but when you accepted the job, you were told that starting time is 8 a.m. Unless you learn otherwise, the smart thing to do is to be there when the day begins officially—perhaps even a few minutes early, if you really want to impress.

The Art of Looking Busy

Bring something to read so you can look busy while everyone else is strolling in, lingering at the coffee machine, and subtly sizing you up.

What you read says something about you, so avoid the comics and books about anarchy or annihilation of the establishment. A newspaper is perfect; if you really want to do this right, make sure it is turned to the business pages.

Dress Up a Little

If this office has a casual dress code, you needn't wear your best interview suit. Still, it is a good idea to dress extra smart on your first day, because first impressions are lasting.

To dress for a first day in almost any office, follow these guidelines:

- If everyone wears suits, wear a good one—possibly your best. Make it your most conservative, if that is called for, or your most fashionable.
- If everyone wears casual pants and/or skirts and shirts, dress up this basic outfit with a sweater, vest, jacket, or scarf that upgrades the outfit just a bit.
- If some but not all men wear ties, wear one today even if you know you'll never wear one again.

Guidelines: Dressing Don'ts

Here are some things *not* to wear on your first day at a new job:

- blue jeans
- T-shirt
- sundress
- unusual hat
- sneakers or sandals
- deep red, black, or blue nail polish
- unusual hair color (blue, purple, etc.)
- pierced jewelry (except earrings)

Maintenance Matters

Your shoes should be polished—leather shoes are much more appropriate than sneakers—and your clothes fresh pressed from the dry cleaner. Pay special attention to your personal grooming today, too: Floss your teeth, use deodorant, and make sure your nails are clean and filed smooth.

What's the real purpose of all this extra effort? In addition to giving your coworkers reason to form a good impression about you, you'll be convincing the guy who hired you that made the right choice after all. Remember, the last time he or she saw you, you were dressed and groomed to the hilt for the job interview.

WHEN THE BOSS ARRIVES

Something odd happens after you're hired, and it usually starts on the first day.

When you were going through the hiring process, your prospective boss couldn't flatter you enough. You were the cat's meow! But between the last interview and your first day at work, the balance of power shifted back. No matter how hard the boss wooed you during the interview stage, now that you're on staff, you're just another worker who has to pay his or her dues to earn respect.

To earn your boss's respect, try using these ideas:

- **Stand up.** Greet your boss on your feet when he or she addresses you for the first time.
- **Shake hands and say hello.** Then, wait for the boss to take the initiative in conversation.
- **Keep the conversation relevant.** Don't say how hard it was to find the office or how shockingly long your commute was— the boss doesn't want to hear this, now or ever.
- **Take your cue from the boss's mood.** If it's harried, don't contribute to that state of mind; if it's businesslike, you do the same; if it's chatty, respond accordingly.
- **Act pleased at any suggestion.** If your boss suggests that another employee walk you through the first day, say that you're delighted to have a chance to meet a coworker. Never act disappointed over the fact that you are being handed off to someone else.
- **Show initiative.** The boss will love you for it. If you need to go to the human resources office but your boss doesn't have time to take you for another hour, offer to find it yourself. If you have nothing to do and your

boss asks you to wait at your desk, make yourself look busy—read the business pages again. Ask if there is some work-related material you could study. Or, turn on the computer and make yourself look busy that way; this might be a good time to take a computer tutorial on unfamiliar software.

FIRST STOP: HUMAN RESOURCES

Human resources—or HR, still called personnel in some companies—is usually the first stop of any new employee. If you work for a large company, HR may consist of an entire department. If you work for a small company, however, you may be handed off to a one-person HR department without even realizing it. The boss's secretary or someone else may do double duty in this capacity.

In any event, you will help someone set up an employment record for you. This involves filling out tax forms, medical forms (if your employer offers health insurance), and a sheaf of other papers. To facilitate this process, bring your Social Security card, a copy of your résumé, and any other papers that might help you complete these forms.

Human Resources and You

It's important to look out for your own interests during your first meeting with HR. If your boss promised you three weeks' vacation during your job interview, and the HR representative insists that as a new employee you are only entitled to two weeks, now is the time to iron this out—tactfully, of course.

If there is a disagreement about the terms of your employment, calmly inform the HR person what you were promised. You don't want this person to report back to your boss that you have an attitude problem, and if you are lucky, you will get this person to discuss the length of your vacation with your new boss.

Drug and Alcohol Tests

You may be asked to submit to drug and alcohol tests as a condition of your employment. It is legal for companies to do these tests, provided they are administered randomly.

No one likes them, and your first instinct may be to refuse. However, this may not be in your best interests, especially if you hope to work for this company for a long time. Consider that if you refuse, even if you have nothing to hide you will

---

?? Question & Answer

Q: I have to undergo a medical exam for my new job, but I have a medical condition I'd rather not have people know about—at least not until I've proved myself on the job—so I'm worried. Should I take the human resources person into my confidence and explain my fears?

A: There's no need to reveal anything to the human resources person. Even when a medical exam is work related or for insurance purposes, the patient-doctor relationship is still confidential.

You are right to want to prove yourself first, so there's really no need to confide your problem to anyone except the doctor until you are ready to do so.

---

look as if you do. The best advice I could give you is to take the test now and then arrange to testify before the U.S. Congress the next time they try to pass a law banning such tests.

As an aside, you may be interested to know that if you fail a drug or alcohol test as a newly hired employee, you probably will be fired—or you will probably not be not hired, if passing the test was a condition of employment—without being given a chance to explain. Some employers pay for employee drug rehabilitation, but this perk invariably goes to long-term employees, not new hires.

SECOND STOP: YOUR NEW OFFICE

Whether your office is an open cubicle or a grand suite with an impressive view of the city, it is going to be your home for some time, you hope. Therefore, you should settle in without complaint, regardless of the size or the view (or lack of).

Office Decor

Most people spend more time at work than they do at home. Even so, you shouldn't make the mistake of thinking of your office as "home," at least not when it comes to decorating. You can do anything you want to with your home, but the same cannot be said for your office. Rules that you do not apply at home apply here; some of these are written, some not. Observe your new environment and figure out what you can and cannot do when it comes to decorating your office.

Start by taking note of what your fellow workers have done to their offices. Pay special attention to those who work on the same job level as you, because many companies have rank-related restrictions about office decor. One major retailer, for example, has a splendid collection of Early American art, but definite rules apply regarding who gets to hang what. Executives display paintings, mid-level managers show off drawings and prints, and low-level employees must settle for reproductions.

Also take note of the extremes of office decor, because frankly, this is something you won't want to emulate. Most offices have a rebel or an eccentric who announces his or her individuality via office decor. Such people are often tolerated but rarely promoted.

Careful observation should cue you in to what you can do. Do people have plants? knick-knack displays? framed pictures of their families? posters or cartoons on their office doors? All of these practices vary from one office to the next, so it is to your advantage to figure out how to fit in.

What Does the Boss Like?

It's also wise to take a reading of your boss's decorating style before you begin to decorate your own space. Some bosses like their employees to settle into their offices and make them homey, whereas others prefer to cultivate a more stark, businesslike atmosphere. Your boss's office offers the best clue to what is considered acceptable.

Go Slow!

After you have figured out what kind of decorating you can do, take it slow. After a couple of weeks on the job, if all goes well, add a photograph or post an amusing cartoon on the door. Then, add other personal touches, one by one.

Decorating for Customers

If you will be meeting with customers in your office, this should influence how—and how much—you decorate your office. A quirky object or two can be enormously helpful in initiating conversation with a stranger. Mary, for example, treated herself to an unusual paperweight from a museum store to celebrate her first job. It has sat on her desk ever since. It brings her luck (she believes) and also amuses both customers and coworkers.

A word of caution: Don't create an office environment so quirky that it amuses customers too much or makes them feel uncomfortable.

Decorate without Offense

Here are a few tips on office decor and decorating:

- **Avoid cute objects.** They are too youth-oriented and lack the seriousness required for the workplace.
- **Be careful with humor.** There's a wonderful episode of *Seinfeld* in which Elaine tapes an obscure cartoon to her door and makes it an acid test for all who pass by. This can backfire, especially if your boss doesn't get the joke.
- **Respect your coworkers.** Pass on anything that could be construed offensive to a person of another race, ethnicity, religion, gender, or sexual preference.
- **Keep personal items out of sight.** Nail files and clippers, perfume, nail polish, combs and hairbrushes, hosiery, extra shoes, and makeup should be hidden away. Even a small kit containing personal items should be stored in a drawer when not in use.
- **Stash shopping bags.** Take them out only when you go shopping on your lunch hour or after work.
- **Hang up your coat.** Don't leave it draped it over a chair.
- **Throw away waste.** Dispose of food and beverage containers when you are finished eating or drinking.
- **Keep desktop clutter to a minimum.** Some people think a messy desk is a sign of genius; most bosses think geniuses ought to be able to work in a tidy environment.

Guidelines: Introductions

Here's how to get an "A" in introductions:

- Stand when you meet someone for the first time.
- Look that person in the eye.
- Smile!
- Say the person's name clearly and repeat yours clearly.
- Hold out your hand and grasp the other person's hand firmly.
- Don't make your handshake too limp or too tight.
- Shake only once or twice—don't pump it, and don't grasp it with both hands. Don't pull away, though, when others do this to you.

MEETING AND GREETING

In an ideal world, someone would escort you through every minute of your first day on the job, introducing you to everyone and explaining who does what. In the real world, you'll have to field the curiosity yourself most of the time.

When you meet your coworkers, do a few things so you will be remembered:

- **Stand up and introduce yourself.** Whenever someone says hello, state your name clearly, using your first and last name.
- **Say what you do.** For example, say, "I'm working for Mr. Jones in accounting."
- **Extend your hand in greeting.** These days, it is considered appropriate for men, women, secretaries, and the company president to shake hands.
- **Don't be quick to use first names.** It may not be obvious whether someone is your age (and remember it can be hard to tell) and rank.
- **Show an interest in others.** Ask them what they do and who they work for.

A Rose by All Its Names

Figuring out what to call people, especially when you're young and new at work, can be tricky. Call someone who's just turned 40 "Sir" or "Ma'am," and you may earn that person's eternal dislike. Call the company president by his or her first name, even if he or she is only slightly older than you, and you may have presumed far too much.

There are several ways to solve the name problem. One is not to call people anything until you figure out what they prefer. Because this is a less friendly approach, as soon as you learn people's names, be sure to use them when speaking with them.

Alternately, err on the side of formality, and call everyone "Mr." or "Ms."—or "Miss" and "Mrs.," if this seems to be the thing to do in your office.

In most offices the name problem shakes down pretty quickly. You listen to what everyone else does, and then follow suit. If after some time you still haven't found what you should call a person, ask. He or she will surely appreciate your sensitivity.

> ### 🔍 CASE HISTORY
>
> When Ron was 21 years old and just out of school, he got his first job working at a library in a small town. The librarian, Joan Brooke, was very approachable. Ron noticed that everyone who came into the library called her by her first name.
>
> Ron couldn't bring himself to do the same, partly because he had just met her and partly because she reminded him of his grandmother. Ron worried about being too stiff and formal, because they worked closely together all day.
>
> Eventually, Ron solved his problem by developing his own nickname for Mrs. Brooke. He called her Mrs. B., which they both found endearing and slightly informal, yet respectful.

Dealing with Personalities

Every office has its oddballs and eccentrics that you'll need to decide how to deal with, usually from the first day on the job. If the clerk in the mailroom talks the ear off everyone he meets but is basically a sweet guy, your coworkers will think you're kind if you take a few minutes to chat with him. If he really wastes too much time, however, you may want to set an early precedent by tactfully cutting him off.

Unfortunately, not all the office "personalities" are so well-intentioned or harmless, and not all are easy to spot at first. That said, it is smart to maintain a little distance and to be wary of instant intimacy when it is offered the first day you are on a new job.

Be cautious of people who sidle up to you and immediately want to become your best friend or, worse, insist on filling you in on office politics. Among these ranks, unfortunately, often are the office gossip, the establishment hater, and the rebel—people you probably won't want to associate yourself with.

It takes time to take the measure of any person, and your best bet is to go slowly with all office friendships. Decline offers of after-work drinks or even lunch until you figure out who's who. Once you settle in, you'll have time to figure out who your friends and allies are.

Be Nice to Everyone

Even though you'll want to be a little cautious about forming friendships, it is also important to be nice to everyone. It is difficult to know right away who has the boss's ear, who wields real power despite a low-level job title, or who is the company president's wife's cousin.

If you are nice to everyone, when you decide to build alliances, you will have a bigger roster to choose from.

THE TRIAL

Don't let your guard down right away! All new employees are on probation, whether they know it or not. In some offices, this is a formal period of varying duration, but even when there isn't a formal probation, a new employee's first several weeks are an informal trial period.

The probationary period typically lasts from three months to one year. It is over when your boss formally meets with you to assess your job performance. If there is no formal assessment, it is over when he relaxes with you and begins to treat you like a member of the team instead of the "new person." Lacking any of these indicators, it is safe to assume you are off probation when you receive your first raise.

And Remember ...

- Show up on time for your first day at a new job.
- Look good, so you make a good first impression.
- Act interested and eager to be there, and express your pleasure when others offer to help you out or show you around.
- Be polite to everyone you meet.
- Go slowly in building relationships.
- Don't settle into your office too quickly.
- Remember: You're on probation for a while on any new job.

CHAPTER | 3

DRESSING WELL AT WORK

Every office has a dress code, whether it is official or not. Even if a dress code is spelled out in the employee handbook, there are always some unwritten rules that you are left to decipher on your own.

Dressing well—and appropriately—for work is important. It helps you fit in and speeds your acceptance by your coworkers, management included. It definitely can help you get promoted. Sadly, the reverse is true as well: Inappropriate dress will hold you back.

DRESSING FOR CUSTOMERS

In addition to impressing your boss and coworkers, your clothing also matters when you have contact with customers or any other time you are representing the company.

If your work puts you in touch with clients, it is important that you dress well and in pretty much the same fashion as your customers.

People like to feel a kinship with the people they work with and, more specifically, those they do business with.

Upgrading Your Wardrobe

One difficult problem most people face at least once in their work lives is how to reasonably and inexpensively upgrade a wardrobe from school to the workplace. Few people can afford to go out and buy a closet full of new clothes, yet, let's face it—most of the clothes that are fine for school don't quite make the grade at work.

Fortunately, there are some interesting and cost-saving ways to work yourself up to a good office wardrobe. For starters, it helps to plan for the long term. Build up your work wardrobe gradually, over two or three years, not during your first year in the working world.

Buying Classics

Use your first few paychecks to invest in one or two good, classic articles of clothing. The word *invest* is not used lightly here, because you should buy some pieces that you'll be able to wear for several years. "Classic" does not have to mean boring. It's okay to spend your money on one unusual or spectacular piece later, provided you love it enough to wear it for a while and that it goes with several different outfits.

Depending on your individual needs, some good first buys might be a blazer and some well-made shirts, blouses, or knit jerseys.

The Basics

Next, add to your classic pieces with some basics. These are clothes you can wear over and over, with many different outfits, without anyone noticing. Unlike the classic purchases, basics are intended to blend into the woodwork. With one sharp jacket and two very nice shirts, you can wear the same skirt or pants two or three times a week. This is how basics work.

Your first basics should be good pants or skirts in dark or neutral colors such as black, brown, or navy blue.

Quality versus Quantity

When building a work wardrobe, try to think quality over quantity. This may sound strange to someone who needs an entirely new wardrobe, but you'll have time later to concentrate on expanding your wardrobe via a few very fashionable

Guidelines: Showing Off Status

No two ways about it, on some level, how you dress for work is always a somewhat competitive undertaking. Here, then, are five fool-proof ways to signal status.

- **Wear an expensive yet plain watch.** No diamonds, please. For men, the classiest watch has Roman numerals on its face, is thin, and has a leather band. Women can sport a gold watchband, but the more tailored its style, the classier it is. An inexpensive but well-designed watch can also have a certain cachet.
- **Wear less rather than more jewelry.** Make it good, or real, if you can afford to do so. One good pair of gold earrings or pearl studs that you wear every day indicate more status than a different pair of costume earrings for each day of the week.
- **Buy one extravagantly upscale item of clothing.** This might be a trench coat, a winter coat, or perhaps a blazer. It will make everything else you wear look more expensive.
- **Buy good shoes, purses, and briefcases—preferably made of leather.** These items add instant class. Besides, if you buy good ones, you won't have to buy new ones nearly so often.
- **Women should buy quality scarves, and men should buy expensive ties.** These accessories are always noticed and confer instant status. Buy what appeals to you, not designer labels meant to impress.

yet inexpensive items. For now, keep the focus on upgrading, because a few good pieces will make everything you already own look better.

Once you've spent most of your hard-earned money on high-quality basics, you can begin to fill in with less expensive, more fashion-oriented clothes. A shirt or a knit jersey, for example, doesn't have to be expensive if you wear it under a good blazer. If you're in a field where you don't have to look conservative or where you must look very fashionable, this is where you splurge on what's new and trendy.

Accessorize, Accessorize

Use accessories to upgrade across the board and make all your clothes look appropriate for work. A cheerful scarf or a colorful tie is a great touch. Jewelry also dresses up clothes. Major accessories, such as shoes, purses, and briefcases also can help to build the kind of look you need for work.

Start building an accessories wardrobe in much the same way that you are building a clothing wardrobe.

Pulling It All Together

There is no need to discard your old clothes as you buy new ones. Once you have upgraded with some office gear, begin to mix and match. Wear your new clothes with your old school clothes. You'll be pleased to discover how much the great-looking new jacket dresses up your old khakis, denim skirts, and even jeans.

CHOOSING WELL-MADE CLOTHES

Quality work clothing costs four to five times that of casual or weekend clothes, so you'll want to be sure you're getting quality when you pay for it. Here are some hints to help you spot well-made clothes:

- **Sleeves should be set in smoothly.** Setting in sleeves is the hardest part of making a jacket or coat, and well-done ones are an invariable sign of quality. Rule out garments with puffy areas or wrinkles or pleats where the sleeve joins the body of the garment.
- **Plaids, stripes, and other patterns should match.** This means that if the material is flowered and a flower has been cut through the middle to make a seam, then the other side of the seam should consist of the other half of the flower—matched perfectly along the seam. Unmatched patterns are a major flaw of cheap clothing.
- **Stitching should be tight and even.** Check all seams. Stitches should be about ¼ inch long. Longer stitches are less sturdy.
- **The collar should lay flat.** It should fit smoothly against the back of your neck, not gape or stand away from your body.
- **Vents and back pleats should lay flat.** If they don't, the garment will always look a little too tight.
- **Pants and skirts should fall straight from your body.** Pants should break over the tops of men's shoes. (Note: Most American men wear their pants too short.) The length of women's pants varies with current fashion.

- **Buy the size that fits you.** Quality clothing can be altered, but it can rarely be altered more than two sizes. Don't rationalize buying the wrong size because it's on sale, the last one, or any number of other excuses that salespeople might use to get you to buy something you'll never like.

The Acid Test: Movement

Before you buy a garment, always test it by moving around in it. Make sure you like how it looks when you sit, that you can easily raise your arms, and that you can move around comfortably in it. If you can't, don't buy it. It will never feel comfortable, and you will never look comfortable wearing it.

 Guidelines: Getting a Great Fit

To make sure that your clothes fit you well, have them altered from time to time by a professional tailor or seamstress. To get the most out of a fitting, be prepared:

- **Shoes:** Wear the same shoes you plan to wear when wearing the skirt or pants. Shoes can dramatically affect the length of a finished garment.
- **Hosiery:** Wear pantyhose or the same kind of socks you will wear when you wear the clothes.
- **Posture:** Stand up straight, but not artificially so. Keep your arms at your sides while the garment is being fitted. This will help to make you even on both sides, something few of us are naturally.
- **Attitude:** Listen to your fitter. He or she undoubtedly fits a lot clothes and can be counted on to advise you regarding sleeve and pants length.

DRESSING LIKE A GROWN-UP

Many young or inexperienced workers make the mistake of dressing too young for the workplace. In these days of youth worship, even some older, experienced workers have lost sight of what is appropriate and inappropriate as office wear.

If you groan at the thought of not flashing your best asset—your youth—or at not being the office trendsetter, don't worry. Dressing your age once meant dressing dowdy, but this is no longer true. Besides, on weekends, you can wear any outrageous outfits you choose. At work, you'll fare better and get promoted faster if you dress to impress the people who make the decisions.

Not dressing like a grown-up, in fact, can be a costly mistake. The price may be that you don't get the promotion you covet or the raise you deserve. Even worse, you're often the last to know what is holding you back. Most bosses who will readily point out problems related to your work will be reluctant to tell you that your style of dress is inappropriate for the workplace.

Many offices have their own guidelines for what is considered appropriate dress, but here are some rules that apply in any office:

- **No low-cut tops.** A woman doesn't look serious about her work if she wears revealing clothing. Few male bosses will mention this, however, for fear of being accused of sexual bias. Men can make the same mistake: Shirts unbuttoned to the waist and revealing "muscle shirts" never advanced anyone's career—even if worn only on dress-down Fridays.
- **Skip the miniskirts.** Besides the distraction they cause, short skirts aren't practical for office wear. It's impossible to sit comfortably, let alone do much of anything in a skirt that barely covers one's torso.
- **Avoid very long skirts unless they're in style.** Whether or not you should do this depends on the climate of your workplace. If it is rather conservative, then skirts that range too far from your kneecaps may be inappropriate.
- **Wear dark-toned colors, at least in your basic clothes.** Keep bright colors and interesting patterns for your accessories—ties or scarves—or even your shirt or blouse. These days, dark clothes are the mark of a well-dressed, up-and-coming employee.
- **Save the unusual nail colors for the weekend.** You know that black nail polish doesn't slow down your fingers as they move over the keyboard, but it may irritate an uptight boss. Why take the chance?
- **Choose a hair style that fits in with your coworkers.** This applies to men and women. The best way to figure out what's okay is to check out how others wear their hair. In conservative workplaces, men may wear their hair short, so long tresses tied back in a ponytail might not go over very well. If no women have bleached-blonde hair with one-inch roots, you might want to pass on this look as well.

- **Wear clothing that fits.** Even when it's in style, unusually loose or unusually tight clothing is a badge of the youth culture and a dead giveaway that you don't consider yourself an adult. Save these looks for the weekends.
- **Put away the class ring or club jewelry.** It's a sure sign that you just got out of school.

GET HELP IF YOU NEED IT

If you suspect that your style of dress is a problem in your workplace, ask a friend to give you an honest opinion. You also could invest a few dollars in some professional advice.

How They Work

A few hours spent with a professional shopper can be a great investment. She or he can help you pull together just the look you need. Professional shoppers either charge by the hour or take a percentage of the price of the clothes you buy. Admittedly, most of their clients are executives who spend a lot of money on their clothing, but any professional shopper worth his or her salt ought to consider it a rewarding challenge to spend a couple of hours with someone who is new to the job scene. Ask for a per-hour fee or a package price.

WEARING THE RIGHT LOOK

Even if your clothes are from the same place your boss shops, you'll also need to learn *how* to wear them. Most offices have a few folk customs about dress. For example, do the men in your office rarely shed their jackets or roll up their sleeves, or do they remove their jackets as soon as they get to work, but meticulously put them on again to go to lunch, even on the hottest summer day? If so, you'll undoubtedly want to follow this practice. Women may follow this practice, too.

Do people dress down on days when they are not seeing clients or customers? In some offices, people do this, while in others, no distinctions are made. Do people bring a sweater or vest to work and wear it after they take off their jackets? Do they wear bright colors or stick with fairly sedate ones? In most offices, what people wear and how they wear it amounts to a uniform. It's up to you, the new employee, to figure out how to fit in—in both choosing and wearing your clothes.

DRESS-DOWN FRIDAYS

One of the most confusing, vague office customs to arise in years is what is commonly—and sometimes euphemistically—called dress-down Fridays. In many companies, management permits the wearing of casual clothes on Fridays. However, even offices that do this may have a host of unwritten rules about what's acceptable.

Jennifer, a young lawyer in a very button-down firm, for instance, heard about dress-down Fridays during the first week on her new job. Unfortunately, she didn't wait to find out what this meant.

On her first Friday, Jennifer showed up in a low-cut lacy top because she and her husband were going out to dinner to celebrate their anniversary. Jennifer figured if she could dress casually, she could dress any old way. She learned differently, though. The stares—some subtle, some not—were enough to make her painfully aware of her mistake by noon, especially when she was called into an impromptu meeting with a prospective client.

Jennifer was so appalled by this experience that she refused to participate in dress-down Fridays for a good six weeks. By then, she realized that casual dress in her law firm was still pretty dressy by her standards. Men wore sports jackets, and women wore pants instead of skirts, along with expensive cashmere sweaters—accessorized with pearls, no less.

It is no small irony of dress-down Fridays that many people report that they have to buy special clothes to wear. In many offices, dress-down Fridays are just as competitive as any other work day. For this reason, it is a good idea to wear regular office dress the first few weeks on a new job so you can get an idea of what your office considers "casual."

PERSONAL GROOMING

If your personal hygiene habits leave anything to be desired, even the best-fitting, most expensive clothes in the world won't make a good impression. Good grooming is a snap if you follow a few basic guidelines:

- **Bathe often.** Americans customarily bathe once a day, which many Europeans consider too often. Nevertheless, it's pretty hard to beat a fresh-scrubbed look at work.
- **Use a deodorant or deodorant/antiperspirant.** Whether you think you need it or not, use it. Unforeseen tense situations will come up, and you will be sorry if you aren't properly prepared.
- **Groom your nails regularly.** Your coworkers may not notice if you do, but they surely will if you don't. Wash your hands frequently during the day, especially after you do any kind of dirty work (e.g., changing the toner cartridge in the office printer).
- **Make sure your clothes are clean.** Dry clean wools and cottons regularly. (Yes, cotton can be laundered, but think about dry cleaning the cotton you wear to work. It always looks better when it is professionally dry cleaned.)
- **Keep your clothes in good repair.** Sew on missing buttons and fix hems as soon as they need it. Never wear a garment that needs to be mended.
- **Wear tops and shirts only once.** Few things make so nice an impression as a crisp, clean shirt.
- **A polished, well-heeled look will go far.** Clean and polish your shoes regularly. Many shoes today don't need to be reheeled, but they should still be watched for signs of wear. When they begin to keel like a sailboat on a windy day, it's time to either repair the heels or replace the shoes.

GENDER-ORIENTED DRESSING TIPS

There aren't so many differences as there once were between men's and women's dress. If conservative suits are the order of the day in an office, these days women as well as men are likely to wear them. Still, most women do try to look both professional and feminine at work. Here are a few hints.

Special Hints for Women

- **Invest in suits of conservative colors.** Save the color for accessories and tops. Your clothes will look stylish longer.
- **Buy color-coordinated office clothes.** Then, you can mix and match them to create more outfits.
- **Choose well-made clothes that fit well.** Invest in the best you can afford.
- **Accessorize upward.** Good leather shoes, a stylish leather purse, or tasteful jewelry can make a not-so-expensive outfit look better than it is.
- **Go light on the jewelry.** A watch is standard, and think about adding only one or two more pieces. Wear small jewelry if you work in a conservative environment.
- **Wear very little perfume.** Consider a light, sporty fragrance rather than a heavy, romantic scent.
- **Keep makeup low-key.** Less is more in office life.

Special Hints for Men

- **Buy clothing in conservative colors.** As is the case with women's clothes, your clothes will stay in fashion longer.
- **Show personality in your choice of shirts, ties, and socks.** This is where you can get creative.
- **Buy the best shirts you can afford.** After all, in most offices, men shed their jackets and walk around in their shirt sleeves all day, so shirts are what show.
- **Invest in a good pair of shoes.** Choose conservative ones if you wear a suit. (Running shoes with a suit, on either men or women, instantly undermine an outfit.)
- **Wear little jewelry.** Perhaps only a watch and a ring will do if you work in a conservative field. Earrings and necklaces, while at times fashionable on men, can undermine a good look.
- **Use deodorant.** Apply it even if you don't like it or don't think you need it. You do, especially during hot summer days when you've already sweated a gallon before you even get to work.
- **Don't use cologne.** Once acceptable, this practice has become passé. If it comes back into style, that's a different matter, but unless you're very discreet with after shave or cologne, go to work unscented.

Case History

Jane started her career working for a youth music magazine, where she picked up an appetite for very fashion-forward, expensive clothes and a look—complete with body piercing and blue hair—to go along with them. Not surprisingly, this look put her in good stead when she worked in the music industry. Even so, she was one of the tamer dressers among her colleagues.

When Jane switched to paralegal work a few years later, she couldn't understand why she failed to win the promotion she had been promised when she was hired. She longed to break out of the paralegal pool and work with one lawyer so she could pick up an area of expertise that would in turn make her still more promotable.

Only when Jane asked her boss to tell her point-blank why she was not getting the promised promotion did she learn, to her surprise, that she was being held back by her personal style. Clearly, her clothes were creative and expensive, her boss assured her, but the short skirts, nose ring, and blue-tinted hair simply weren't something the law firm felt it could wave in front of its clients.

Initially, Jane was aghast and loath to give up a look she loved. Fortunately, though, a friend suggested that she consult with a personal shopper. This woman persuaded Jane that she could tone down her look to make it suitable for her workplace and still project her personality.

Today, Jane wears a funkier hairstyle than she wore before—a crewcut!—but she has lost the blue hair. She wears "straight" suits on days when she meets with clients and still amuses the office with totally off-the-wall outfits on days when she knows she will not be working with clients.

Jane has become so good at her job that the boss who once refused to pull her out of the paralegal pool is now urging her to go to law school.

And Remember ...

- Build a work wardrobe steadily and slowly, buying the best clothing you can afford.
- Learn to spot well-tailored clothes that fit you well; insist on buying nothing less.
- Make sure your grooming is impeccable.
- Every office has a dress code as well as a dress uniform. Figure out what it is where you work, then follow it.

CHAPTER | 4

THE EMPLOYEE-BOSS RELATIONSHIP

Everyone has to figure out how to get along with the boss—sometimes with several bosses, because the lines of authority are not clearly drawn in every company.

Bosses have real power. They hire and fire. They recommend you for promotion. They control raises. They supervise your work, which means they can send more—or less—interesting assignments your way. Knowing how to act so as not to offend your superiors is important if you want to be successful in your job. Knowing how to make them happy is what gets you noticed and promoted.

SHOWING RESPECT

A good beginning is to understand and respect the boss's power. A few basic guidelines will help you do this:

- **Call your boss what he or she prefers.** Whether it's Mr. Jones or Jim, respect your boss's wishes.

- **Let your boss take the lead.** This doesn't mean you can't show initiative, just that your boss generally gets to go first. Let your boss say what's on his or her mind before you say what's on yours.

- **Put your boss first in small things.** If you're on the phone and your boss comes into your office, end the call. If you're chatting with a coworker—even if you're talking about work—and you see that your boss wants to talk to you, cut your chat short.

- **Don't do things that you know irritate your boss.** This would seem obvious, but sometimes bosses really are like parents to young or inexperienced workers, and the urge to play out your passive aggressions on your boss will be larger than you might imagine. So, if you know your boss hates it when people arrive late to work or take longer than one hour for lunch, the solution is simple: Don't do these things.

- **Be friendly, but don't overdo it.** Don't discuss your personal problems with your boss or assume you can drop in uninvited to chat about the weather. Limit your exchanges to polite conversation and work-related topics until you know your boss well enough to know whether he or she has any interest in your personal life or, for that matter, any interest in sharing his with you.

- **Stand in your boss's office until he or she invites you to sit down.**

- **Invite your boss to sit down immediately in your office.**

- **Don't handle or touch objects on your boss's desk.** Don't study them openly from your seat. Don't acknowledge them unless you are invited to do so.

❓ Question & Answer

Q: I'm only 23, and I keep calling my boss "Sir" even though he's only 35. I know this drives him crazy, but I can't seem to stop myself.

A: This *can* drive someone crazy. As a general rule of thumb, in these days of casual manners, it's better not to call anyone "Sir" who isn't clearly old enough to be pleased by it.

As for your present situation, the first step is to let him know that you know it's a minor irritation. Say something like, "I know you hate it, and I'd like to stop it, but my mouth won't let me. I'm working on it, believe me." Then make a joke when it happens. Salute or say, "Yes, sir, bossman, whatever." Laugh, and hope he does the same.

- **Don't waste your boss's time.** This is perhaps the most important hint of all. Bosses usually are busy people, so don't take up their time unless you have a legitimate business question that no one else can answer.

EARNING YOUR OWN RESPECT

You'll not only want to respect the boss but also make sure he or she respects you. This is the key to getting interesting and important work assignments, to say nothing of raises and more responsibility.

Respect takes time to build, so when you're new on a job, remember that it won't come immediately. In many offices, you will encounter an invisible barrier that holds you back until your prove yourself—or until you're off probation. Smart bosses know better than to get chummy with new employees before they have proven their worth. They hold something in reserve because they know they may have to fire that person.

For your first few months in a new job, therefore, assume that your boss doesn't trust you. Your boss will be watching your work habits to see whether you arrive at work on time, whether you're willing to stay late when necessary, whether you're a team player, and how well you do your work—in short, whether you're the kind of employee he or she wants to keep on the team and possibly take up through the ranks.

Respect is a complex emotion, especially the way it operates in the workplace. A boss can respect you but not particularly like you—and you'll soon discover, if you haven't already, that the reverse is true: You can respect a boss you don't like, or even fear.

Paying Dues to Earn Respect

You need to earn a boss's respect on two levels. The first is the nitty-gritty everyday level, where you simply show that you are a good worker and take your job seriously. The second is a higher level that will make you look like someone who should be given added responsibilities and promotions. To earn this kind of respect,

- **Arrive on time.** It shouldn't matter that you arrive 10 minutes late if you do your job well, and it's easy to feel belligerent about this rule. Sometimes it's really tough to get in on time, but promptness really matters. Bosses like to

---

THE RIGHT PROTOCOL

When I go somewhere with my boss, who is the chairman of the board, I'm never sure who should go through the door first or, for that matter, be accorded small courtesies. He's always trying to let me go through doors first—because I'm a woman, I'm sure—yet because he's my boss and the chairman, I feel he should go first. What's the right protocol?

The right protocol on small matters of courtesy has become complicated as more women have entered the workplace. If you've ever watched a group of men go through a doorway, you'll notice that the highest ranking one invariably goes first, and everyone else falls in behind in descending order. Add a woman to the mix, and there's typically a lot of fumbling.

Your boss is clearly signaling to you that he's more comfortable letting you go first, probably because he's old enough to want to feel chivalrous, and there's no reason not to let him.

Most chairmen of the board radiate enough power so people realize who they are. Besides, there are probably other ways you can show deference, such as calling him "Mr. Williams," for example.

---

walk in and see all their employees looking ready to put in a full day's work. Furthermore, if the boss comes in early, it's not a bad idea to do the same—if you're ambitious.

- **Try arriving at work early.** Apart from the edge this may give you in doing your work, this shows genuine eagerness and interest and is a surefire way to impress the boss. Amazingly, coming in even 10 or 15 minutes early is enough to earn you lots of extra points.

- **Act eager—even when you're not.** In all jobs, people have to do jobs they don't particularly want or like to do. If you show a willingness to do these things, your boss will notice and find a way to reward you.

- **Complete assignments on time and with minimal fuss.** This is how you show that you are a go-getter: Do that assignment to the best of your ability, without making a big show of it, and you'll impress your boss in a big way.

- **Turn down nothing.** Refusals are not impressive in the workplace. Take on all the work you can, at least initially, until you've made your mark.

- **Take the initiative.** You should accept all work assignments given to you, but it's also okay for you to take the initiative. When something comes around that you really want to do, volunteer to do it or to work with whomever is doing it. If you wouldn't necessarily be considered for this assignment, arrange to sit down with your boss for a few minutes to pitch yourself as the person for the assignment.

- **Never brood, mope, or whine when things don't go your way.** This behavior is inappropriate in the workplace and only makes you look immature. If you ask for an assignment and don't get it, then work all the harder on whatever assignment you do get, so next time you'll be considered for the big one.

- **Leave your personal problems at home.** One of the biggest mistakes inexperienced workers make is taking their personal problems to work with them. The next biggest mistake is talking too much about their personal lives.

Keep Your Personal Life Personal

Anyone who employs you is primarily interested in whether you are a good worker. To this end, if you start to moan about your nasty divorce, the boss may be empathetic but also begin to worry how much this situation is going to affect your ability to do your job.

In a similar vein, if you go out dancing every night after work and let everyone in the office know it, the boss may start to wonder whether you are too tired to get the job done. He or she may blame mistakes on your late habits, even if this is not the case.

This scenario is the start of a downward spiral from which it may be difficult to recover. The best solution is prevention: Don't talk too much about your personal life or problems when you're at work.

An Overwhelming Personal Problem

Sometimes a personal problem becomes so overwhelming that you cannot keep it out of the workplace. In such situations, it's usually better to let your boss know rather than to let him or her notice your distraction and possibly make the wrong assumption—that is, that you are simply goofing off.

If a problem is serious enough, you may want to meet with your boss to discuss the difficulty, but sometimes it's a wiser move to let him or her know in a more subtle way. If at all possible, try not to discuss personal problems until you have arrived at some solution and can offer some assurance that your difficulties are under control and will not affect your ability to do your job.

> ## 🔍 CASE HISTORY
>
> Joan was in the middle of a messy divorce and could barely drag herself to work each day. She felt teary two or three times a day and went off to the ladies' room to cry. Her boss noticed her red eyes, and invited her into his office to talk.
>
> Although Joan was close to collapsing and telling her seemingly empathetic boss every bad thing that was happening in her life, she wisely restrained herself. She told her boss only that she was having some personal difficulties and that her marriage had recently broken up. She added that she was grateful to have her job and could assure him that this would not take a toll on her work.
>
> Even though Joan wasn't performing up to snuff, her boss cut her some slack—he was impressed with her display of confidence in discussing her problem with him. Also, because of her honest, level-headed approach, he was convinced that she would never take advantage of the situation. Most bosses like to be reassured about such things.

PRIVACY AT WORK

It is important to understand the lines of privacy in an office. Inexperienced or young workers often do not know how this works.

A boss is always granted a certain degree of privacy that may not apply to fellow workers, simply because you all work so closely together, perhaps in cubicles or shared offices. In contrast, bosses usually have private offices. If they're good managers, they leave their doors open, therefore inviting certain invasions of their privacy.

Still, it is important to respect the boss's privacy:

- **Do not enter.** Don't go into your boss's office when he or she is not there unless you have a good reason to do so. Ask yourself, "Would I be the slightest bit uncomfortable explaining why I am here if my boss were to suddenly walk in?" If the answer is no, then you are okay.
- **Knock.** Many bosses feel they cannot close their doors, even if doing so would help them work better. Consider a half-open door half-closed—a cry for privacy—and knock before entering.

- **Be discreet.** If your boss has to interrupt a meeting with you to take a personal telephone call, ignore what you hear and carry on with what you were doing before the phone rang. If the telephone call becomes prolonged, get up and leave. The boss will appreciate your finesse.
- **No loitering.** Never give the appearance of hanging outside the boss's office to overhear a conversation with another employee or on a telephone call.

On the Subject of Your Privacy...

Nice as it would be if the boss obligingly followed these same rules with you, no one expects this to happen. Depending on the kind of work you do, your boss may not even be able to. The boss, therefore, is entitled to enter your office when you're not there. Furthermore, your boss can read anything on your desk. To be safe, make sure that everything is related to your work.

CRITICISM

One of a boss's least pleasant tasks is to give criticism. One of an employee's least pleasant tasks is to accept it. It is simply not possible that you will always do your job so perfectly that no occasion will ever arise when you must be reprimanded by your boss.

To put criticism in its most positive light, it can help you do your job better. If you aren't doing something right, it's better to be told about it so you have a chance to remedy the situation, rather than to continue doing it wrong, not understanding why you're not getting any praise. Keep in mind that if you are not doing something right, it reflects poorly on your boss. Therefore, it reflects doubly poorly on your boss if he or she doesn't straighten things out with you.

A good boss knows how to offer criticism so you feel no sting. Unfortunately, too many bosses lack this skill. Your job is to take criticism—in whatever form—constructively, in a mature fashion.

Handling Criticism

To put criticism to work for you, remember these points:

- **Always take it seriously.** Never laugh or joke when the boss tells you that you haven't done something correctly or as well as you might.

- **Never deflect or dismiss it.** This isn't the time to say that the woman who sits next to you does the same thing and the boss never gets on her case. Nor is it the time to offer excuses. When a boss offers criticism, he or she wants a situation to improve. Your boss is not interested in why you think it can't—or shouldn't.

- **Ask for examples.** Criticism does you little good if you don't know specifically what you're doing wrong. Always ask for concrete examples when someone criticizes your work.

- **Don't be surprised though if your boss can't give you any examples.** A good boss will be prepared with examples, but many find the act of criticizing an employee so uncomfortable that they aren't able to come up with any. A boss who is criticizing you unfairly won't be able to come up with any examples anyway. It's good to know this, even though you probably shouldn't point this out to your boss.

- **Offer your own examples if you can.** Describe a situation and ask your boss whether this is what he or she is referring to. Your boss will appreciate your even-handedness.

- **Ask how you can improve.** This response shows remarkable initiative, and you will impress your boss with your maturity and willingness to take criticism constructively.

Public Criticism

The worst criticism is criticism that is offered publicly; even when it's mild, it feels like humiliation. The best bosses are either extremely tactful about issuing criticism in public or offer it only in private. There is one situation where your boss is entitled to criticize you publicly: when your mistake makes him or her look bad.

This happened to Sally, who stayed late one night to finish a report that her boss needed the next morning at a meeting. After going home blurry-eyed and showing up early to proofread the report, she inadvertently grabbed an earlier version and had it copied for the meeting. She and her boss discovered this during the meeting with three important customers.

Sally's boss couldn't—and shouldn't—have taken the fall for her mistake. He was entirely appropriate in saying that the mix-up was Sally's fault.

Even when it's right, public criticism still stings at least twice as much as private criticism. Even so, these tips might make it a little bit easier to handle:

- **Stay polite.** Don't snap back at your boss or in any way make him or her look bad. Apologize, and explain how you'll correct the problem, if possible, and that's it.
- **Keep your cool.** Getting emotional won't go over well. Your quivering chin won't win you any lasting sympathy from the boss, even if it wins you a few immediate allies among others in the room. If you have a good cry later, don't do it in front of anyone.
- **Say as little as possible.** Sputtering excuses or offering a long-winded explanation of what you'll do to fix the situation only makes matters worse. Briefly respond if a response is called for, and leave it at that. Or, offer your boss an explanation later in private if he or she is interested.

As a general rule of thumb, the faster you get through a bout of public criticism, the better you and your boss will feel.

THE RIGHT PROTOCOL

At our monthly meeting with the board of directors, my boss ordered me to bring the wrong report. When I did, he chastised me in front of everyone. He often blames others for his mistakes.

I didn't say anything, but now I'm working on a project with another director, who also was at the meeting, and I'd like to let him know that the mistake wasn't my fault. What's the right thing to do?

Normally, the right protocol is that you tell your boss directly that you're unhappy with his or her behavior. Your situation is somewhat trickier, because you now look bad in the eyes of someone else you work for.

In this case, it is in your best interests to say something to the director you're working with now. Try to approach the problem lightly; don't complain or make a formal announcement. Instead, slip it into conversation, perhaps by saying, "Oh, what happened at that meeting. There's another side to that story."

WHAT TO DO WITH A BAD BOSS?

Bad bosses exist, lots of them. Some don't give criticism well; some don't give it at all. Your boss might approach you one day, out of the blue, with a long list of things you have done wrong but never had a chance to correct. He or she may fire you without giving you a chance to respond, or not fire you—but you have to continue working with that person.

It is tricky to handle a truly bad boss (as opposed to one you simply don't like), but it can be done. It also is important to know the difference between a temperamental boss, who you can handle—albeit with kid gloves—and a boss who is unfair and unreasonable.

If your situation is the latter, then the best solution may be to find another job or find yourself a mentor within the company. Such bosses rarely improve, and they can really stymie a career. Meanwhile, do your job as well as you can, because you'll want good recommendations to help you move on. Let other managers notice what a good job you're doing so they will want you to work for them.

When someone is a truly poor manager, others in the company know it and may even offer support to his or her workers. Unfortunately, as long as you work for a bad boss, it's in your best interests to remain loyal—or at least to act loyal—to him or her. All companies value loyalty, and showing loyalty in the face of such adversity will serve you well in the long run, whether you find yourself a new job inside or outside the company.

Finding a New Boss or Mentor

You can approach someone for whom you would like to work, but do this tactfully. Don't complain about your boss, for example. Instead, mention that you find the work the new prospective mentor is doing very interesting. Ask whether he or she needs any help.

Other managers usually can read between the lines of such a request, and they will appreciate your skill in maneuvering around a difficult problem. They also will assume that if you can remain loyal to your present boss, then you are probably a loyal person in general. This will make you a welcome and valued employee.

? Question & Answer

Q: My boss is a woman, and I'm a man. I also am 10 years her senior. Is there anything I can or should do to remind her of this?

A: Remind her of what? It sounds as if you aren't comfortable working with a woman, especially one who is younger than you, but there's nothing you can or should do about it. A woman who happens to be the boss should be treated exactly the same as any other boss—male or female, younger or older—all the time.

COMPLAINING ABOUT OTHERS

Sometimes it becomes necessary to complain to your boss about a colleague. Because management likes to foster at least the illusion of solidarity, there is a chance that this conversation will not make your boss especially happy. So, complaints of this nature require unusual tact.

Before registering a complaint about a coworker, do everything you can to resolve the problem between the two of you, especially if the problem involves any kind of professional rivalry. Go to the person who is troubling you. Explain how you feel and wait to see whether his or her behavior changes. Warn that if things don't change, you plan to go to the boss. Being able to say that you have already gone the extra mile is a point in your favor with the boss.

Second, never complain about anything small. Minor issues, such as who makes the coffee or who goes to reception area to accept packages, should be resolved without the boss's intervention, if possible. Sometimes the best thing you can do is wait until the boss notices a situation like this, even if it means that you do more than your share of work for a while.

Always try to phrase your complaint in a positive way. For example, you might say, "Although Susie is a very good typist, she doesn't file very well, and I'm worried that the files are getting disorganized." Wrapping a complaint in a compliment is a very effective technique. Don't gossip or badmouth the person, even if the boss agrees with you. Do everything you can to maintain a neutral, I'm-sorry-I-have-to-do-this stance.

Be as specific as you can. Offering "Susie doesn't put the files in the right drawer, and this makes it difficult for everyone to retrieve them" is much more effective than "Susie is just the worst filer I've ever seen."

Complaining About Superiors

Complaints about superiors are very difficult to log, because management is invariably biased toward its own kind. The only time you can justifiably complain about superiors is when the issue is very serious, for example, in issues involving sexual harassment, racial prejudice, or stealing from the company.

MENTOR RELATIONSHIPS

A mentor is one of the best things you can have at work. A mentor is someone, usually but not always a superior, who decides to become your guru. He or she will see that you get interesting work, will push for your promotion, and seek to advance your career in other ways, often by aligning it with his or her own.

Mentoring usually occurs because you are good at what you do, but it also can happen because you will be useful to your supporter. Mentor relationships without a solid basis too often degenerate into sexual harassment or some other bad relationship and are best avoided.

When you have a mentor, he or she makes you look good, but you have to do the same. You're really connected to the person who mentors you, so be careful about who becomes your advisor.

Sometimes it's not possible to choose your mentor. Your mentor may just be the next person in line who wants to train you into the job so he or she can move on. However, sometimes you do have a choice. This is the best possible situation, because you can enlist someone who truly respects you and wants to help advance your career.

Choosing your own mentor is a subtle process. People don't often say, "Will you be my mentor?" The relationship emerges over time. It will have a better chance of emerging if you put yourself forward as much as you can, volunteering to work with that person, doing the best possible job, going the extra mile when necessary.

It's also important never to take advantage of your mentor relationship. There is no faster way to lose a mentor than to act like the teacher's pet! This is exactly what you *aren't*. You are, in fact, a highly qualified person with a special advisor who is very aware that he or she is training you for something else.

It may be helpful to keep in mind that ultimately, mentor relationships are as impersonal as almost everything else about office life.

THE IMPERSONALITY OF IT ALL

Strange as this may seem to some workers, the very best boss-employee relationships are those that are strictly business. You both acknowledge that business is what brings you together and that you either have little in common outside work or little interest in pursuing any common interests because you see enough of each other at work.

A strictly business relationship is the healthiest possible situation for both of you, one that goes a long way toward keeping the relationship on an even keel.

And Remember ...

- You have to earn your boss's respect.
- Good workers show their bosses respect and particularly respect his or her privacy.
- Criticism can improve your job performance, so it's important to listen to and accept it.
- Learn to complain tactfully, especially to the boss.

CHAPTER 5

THE SOCIAL SIDE OF TECHNOLOGY

A few years ago, the average office worker had to know only how to type and field phone calls. Today, that same worker must cope with sophisticated phone systems, beepers, fax machines, e-mail—and a new set of behaviors for using them. In this chapter, you will learn how to put your best foot forward with new and old technologies.

USING THE OFFICE TELEPHONE

The telephone is the still the favored form of immediate, person-to-person communication in most offices. Nothing has managed to totally replace it, and many office workers spend a sizeable part of every day using it.

Answering Calls

There are several ways to answer a telephone at work. If the caller has already been vetted by a receptionist or secretary, then you can simply answer by saying your name, as in, "Riley here" or "Sally Jones."

In some businesses, chiefly those that deliver services, you might also add "May I help you?" or "How can I be of service?" Whether you say this will also depend on the style in your workplace, so one good way to find out how to answer the phone in your office is to listen to how others do it, then follow suit.

If no one has vetted the call, then you may feel it necessary to provide more information. You might, for instance, "Accounting, this is Sally Riley speaking. How may I help you?" Keep in mind that some callers find it reassuring, even if they have gone through a receptionist—or, as is more often the case these days, voice mail—to be told that they have at last reached the right place.

The most important thing to keep in mind regarding your telephone behavior is that you are the voice of your company every time you pick up the telephone, whether you are making or taking a call. At home, you can hang up on an aggressive salesperson—or even an angry friend. At work, you're expected to act professionally at all times.

Start by answering all calls promptly. A ringing office phone may annoy your coworkers, and it won't please callers very much, either. At home, the caller may expect that you need some time to get to the phone; at work, you are expected to be sitting at your desk, waiting for the phone to ring.

?? Question & Answer

Q: I work in the accounting department of a big corporation. One of my least pleasant tasks is to track down customers who don't pay promptly. I always take a tough, almost threatening approach for a couple of reasons. One is that I'm young and I worry that it shows in my voice and my telephone manner. The other is that with the clout of such a big company behind me, I can do this. After all, people aren't going to stop doing business with us because they need our product so much. Am I doing the right thing?

A: Your tough-guy approach is causing more wear and tear on your soul than necessary. As long as the customer is not being abusive to you, try for a firm-but-friendly approach. You may be very surprised to find you get far better results.

Making Calls

Most of the same rules that apply to answering the telephone at work also apply to making them. In other words, be courteous, take your time, and speak in a clear voice.

When you call someone else's office, it's helpful and easier on both you and the person you're calling if you announce yourself, even before you're asked to do so. Say to the person who answers the phone, "Hello, this is Jane Riley from ABC Company. May I speak to Mrs. Frank, please?"

You may also facilitate the call by briefly mentioning why you are calling: "I'm returning Mrs. Frank's call" or "Mrs. Frank asked me to call her today."

When Someone Else Answers Your Phone

You'll want to make sure that the person who answers your phone does as gracious a job of it as you would yourself. This is easy to do when the person works directly for you, but somewhat trickier when he or she is the receptionist for the entire company or your entire department.

If you have a secretary or an assistant, simply explain how you would like to have your telephone answered at the outset or when you notice that he or she is doing it differently. If you notice that the company receptionist is curt or nasty to callers, however, it's better and entirely appropriate to mention this to your boss, the receptionist's boss, or someone in human relations. It's not your place to mention it to the receptionist directly, nor will it serve you well in terms of what you need from that person—unless, of course, you can do this with such extreme tact that he or she doesn't even feel reprimanded.

Pleasant as it is to have someone else answering your phone, there are limits to what that person is supposed to do for you. Many people, for example, are uncomfortable lying, even for a coworker. It's not a good idea for you to use a secretary or an assistant to avoid calls. Sooner or later you'll have to take them, so why put someone else on the spot?

It's perfectly acceptable, though, to ask a secretary or an assistant screen your calls when you truly are too busy to talk. Asking someone to do this day in and day out, however, means only that you are avoiding an important aspect of your job.

All-Around Etiquette

Some rules apply no matter whether you're making or taking a call.

Your Telephone Voice

After you get past the greeting, a few other things will make it a pleasant experience to talk with you on the telephone:

- **Control the volume.** Speak in a well-modulated voice—neither too loud nor too soft. Either can make the conversation difficult for the caller.
- **Speak clearly.** This is especially important if you are quoting prices or any other numbers that are important to either of you. It's not a bad idea to repeat important information like this so you're sure that the person on the other end heard you correctly.
- **Take it slow.** Try never to sound rushed, especially when dealing with customers. However busy you may be, your job is to conduct the business's business, and for this you need to sound patient and helpful.
- **Be courteous.** This is actually a fairly big order, because in today's rushed world, you may not always receive the same treatment in return. Customers may call with legitimate—or illegitimate—complaints. They may be angry about something you personally had nothing to do with and perhaps don't even know about. Despite this, you must respond courteously, even on these occasions.

Who Ends It?

In social calls, the caller is the person who ends the telephone call, but in business either party may end the call as soon as the purpose of the call has been met.

The only exception to this is when your boss or some other high-ranking person calls you. Then it's wise on your part to wait until he or she ends the call.

Saying Good-Bye

A misperception floats through the world of business that important people don't have time actually to utter "Good-bye" at the end of a telephone conversation. In truth, really important people, such the CEOs of major corporations or the chairmen of the board, not only say good-bye at the end of telephone conversations but they are often among the politest people you could speak to. Certainly, no matter what your level, nothing leaves a more unpleasant taste than to have someone abruptly hang up after an otherwise pleasant conversation.

Equally annoying is the person who fades away at the end of the call. The caller hears papers rustling or is interrupted by a background conversation that has nothing to do with him, and the person on the other end literally just fades away.

There's a far more elegant and simple way to end a telephone call. Once the business is concluded, simply say that you have to go, thank you, and good-bye. This direct approach is far kinder than fading away or hanging up without concluding the conversation.

Persistence Pays Off

Occasionally, you will have to call someone who doesn't, for whatever reason, want to speak with you. It may be a potential customer who is eluding you because he or she is busy, or a supplier with whom you are about to lodge a complaint.

In either case, you'll still find that courtesy, combined with a heavy dose of persistence, works best. If someone does not take your call, use your politest voice to ask when he or she will be available. This usually melts the hardest receptionist, who, seeing that you are going to be polite about it, will sometimes switch alliances and help get your call through.

CASE HISTORY

Jackie worked as a client coordinator for a small graphic arts company. Her job was to make—and keep—the customer happy. One customer berated her often, especially on the telephone. If he wanted a booking at a certain time and couldn't get it, he took it out on Jackie. Realizing that this customer was a major client, she tended to simply take the abuse and try to work around it.

Finally, Jackie got fed up with this awful treatment. She considered telling off the client but she felt that if she were to get angry, then on some level, he would have won. So, the next time the client started in on her, she took a deep breath and said in her calmest voice, "I'm not going to talk to you when you treat me like this. I'm going to hang up now, but I'll be here. If at any time you see fit to behave in a more professional manner, I'll be happy to work with you."

To Jackie's gratification and mild surprise, the client called back a couple of hours later and very pleasantly made the appointment he needed. Although he continued to be a slightly quarrelsome customer, he never again mounted a full-scale attack against her.

With hindsight, Jackie realized that being polite didn't mean she had to withstand abusive behavior. Furthermore, she learned that there was a polite way to counter extreme rudeness.

When you are told when the person you need to speak to can be reached, say you'll call back at that time, and do it. Once it has been established that your word is good, you will keep calling back, and you're being astonishingly calm and polite about the whole business, then you probably will find your call being put through.

Speaker Phones

One of the least attractive of the new telephone technologies is the speaker phone. It makes the speaker sound as if he or she is standing in a 10-foot crater, and it creates an impersonal distance between the caller and the called—usually, the last thing you want in business.

Avoid using a speaker phone whenever you can. If you must use one for a conference call, for example, start by placing the call with the handset. Explain to the person you're calling that you will be using the speaker phone so several people can participate in the call. Apologize in advance for the poor sound quality, and only then turn on the speaker and hang up the handset.

If you are unnecessarily subjected to a speaker-phone conversation, it is acceptable to politely protest. When someone insists on using one in a two-person call, it's perfectly okay to explain that you're having trouble hearing or to ask whether he or she is calling you from an echo chamber.

Doing Double Duty

Call waiting is rare in big companies, who have more sophisticated multiple-line telephone systems, but some small companies still use it. Both features permit one call to interrupt another call that is already in progress.

The person with call waiting will hear a clicking on the line that will block out whatever the person on the other end of the line is saying. The person on the other end often doesn't hear anything or know that you haven't heard what he said. The two ways of dealing with call waiting are to ignore it, which can be annoying, because it goes on for as long as the third caller lets the phone ring, or to take the second call.

A person with a multi-line phone will either hear a special ring or see a light on the phone set. Then, he or she can decide whether to put the first caller on hold and answer the second call.

If you decide to answer a second call, tell the first person gracefully what's happening, because he or she may not have heard anything. Rather than simply blurting out, as so many people do, "Oh, wait, I'll be back," and then letting the line go silent, try for a softer approach. Say, "Oh, I've got another call. Can you give me a minute to see who it is? I'll be right back." Then, needless to say, make sure that you do come right back. The first caller should never have to hang up in frustration because you didn't get back to him or her in timely fashion or, worse, because you got so involved with the second caller than you forgot or deliberately left the first one dangling.

Voice Mail

Another exciting but taxing new element of office life is voice mail. This technology replaces a live receptionist who fields calls, takes messages, and can actually assist callers. It throws up a big barrier between supplier and customer, but unlike speaker phones, voice mail is inevitable and not something you can do much about.

For the caller, the biggest problem with voice mail is that the message can go on forever. Sometimes, an automated system provides so many options that you can't remember which one you wanted by the time you have to choose. This problem is easily, if belligerently, solved by simply writing down the various possibilities as the computer voice gives them to you. Once you know which extension or phone key to dial for the person you are calling, you can usually override the lengthy message by punching in that number soon after the message starts.

The person with voice mail has to make sure that the system is as user-friendly as possible:

- **Resist the urge to leave a cute or musical message.** Get right down to business! Musical and lengthy messages are barely acceptable on home phones and annoying to a business caller.
- **Make your message brief.** The days are over when people with new technology had to explain it to those who had not encountered it yet. There is no longer any need to elaborate. You needn't explain, "You have reached my Voice Mail. If you leave a message, I'll return your call as soon as possible." It's far kinder to simply state, "Hello, this is Gary Crouse. Please leave a message."
- **Return calls promptly.** Your first line of defense should be to realize how terribly impersonal the system is and make your callers feel more comfortable with the system.

USING CELLULAR PHONES

It has been said that the primary use for cell phones is to call people from a block away to let them know that you're a block away. However, if they have a real use, it's undoubtedly to facilitate the conduct of business, so it's important to know how to use them properly.

If your employer supplies your cellular phone, think of it as something intended only for business use. Each call costs money—whether you place the call or receive it—so the boss won't be happy to see that you chatted with old friends on the other side of the country for an hour and that your mother calls you every couple of hours just to say "Hi." In fact, before accepting the cell phone, be sure you understand how you are expected to use it. Is it so you can be reached on weekends, or when you're traveling for business?

Because cell phone calls are still more expensive than regular calls, many people try to keep calls brief, and most bosses appreciate this gesture. It's also polite to keep calls brief when you're with someone and a cell phone interrupts, just as you would with a regular phone call. You wouldn't let a telephone call interrupt a conversation or a meeting, so don't let a cell phone call do it either. Naturally, the same rules apply if you absolutely must take a call. Excuse yourself and promise to keep the call short.

Another time to keep a cell phone call brief is when you receive it in a public place, such as a restaurant or a store. Few people want to listen to other people's telephone calls while they're eating or enjoying any other form of entertainment.

For the sake of everyone present, make sure your cell phone is turned off when you're at a movie or a live performance. Justifiably, people get downright indignant when entertainment they've paid good money to see is interrupted in this manner. Theaters have begun to ask this of audiences, but even if you aren't asked, remember to turn it off.

With all the emphasis on keeping cell phone calls brief, it's also important to remember to be courteous. You may sound much more abrupt than you would like if you are concerned with keeping your calls short, so remember to apologize before you press the "End" button. Apart from this, all the other rules of telephone use can be safely applied to cell phones.

BEEPERS

Beepers are akin to cell phones in that they make you readily available to the boss, day and night. Increasing numbers of employers are issuing beepers to workers.

If you are issued a beeper, first find out exactly when you are supposed to have it turned on. You may at first be charmed to keep it constantly at your side, but this excitement fades rather quickly, as do midnight calls from work. When you are beeped, respond immediately. Beepers still have a sense of immediacy about them.

In a similar vein, if you are calling someone's beeper number, make sure you have an urgent reason to do so. Beepers normally aren't used for non-urgent office business that could easily be conducted during regular office hours. Save the beeper for something truly urgent—a real emergency.

Using a beeper is easy to do. Simply call the number of the beeper, punch in your phone number, and hang up. The person you beeped will call you back.

Beepers are as offensive as cell phones in certain public situations, so if you can, request a beeper that has a vibration option in addition to the alarm. If you can't do this, then remember to turn off the beeper, if you can, at movies, in restaurants, and in other public venues where the interruption might not be appreciated.

FAX MACHINES

Besides computers, the other machine that has revolutionized office life is the fac simile, or fax, machine. This machine sends an image of a document over the telephone lines. It is simple to use once you know how, and only the slightest amount of mostly protective protocol has sprung up around it:

- **Use a transmittal sheet.** On this cover sheet write the date, sender, recipient, and the number of pages (including the transmittal sheet) that you are sending.
- **Reduce long or wide pages.** Use the fax or a copy machine to reduce your original documents of legal size, for example, to letter size first. That way, you won't lose any copy when the company on the receiving end only has letter-sized paper in its fax machine—as does most of America.
- **Call first if your document is time-sensitive.** Business mail rooms receive faxes all day long, including numerous junk faxes, and a phone call may be needed to alert the recipient that a fax is coming. Most of the time, you can leave this information with a secretary or a receptionist.
- **Request a quick reply if you need one.** Faxes have lost some of their sense of urgency, and no one rushes around anymore to respond to a letter simply because it is faxed.

E-MAIL

E-mail has transformed communication, making it possible for us to be in steady yet somehow fairly remote contact with each another around the clock.

E-mail transmittals—it would be too much to call these communications letters—are typically written in a kind of shorthand in which the writer pays little or no attention to spelling and grammar. Most of us just spew out the message without bothering to look it over.

Unfortunately, this marvelous informality is sometimes the last thing you need in a business setting. So perhaps the first and most important rule of using e-mail at work is to use it with some degree of formality. Here are some ways to do this:

- **Check your spelling and grammar.** Use the spell-check feature if you have one, especially when you write to someone who doesn't know you.
- **Use a formal greeting.** Treat e-mail messages as business letters.
- **Omit the date and formal heading.** This information will be noted—to the minute—in your message header.
- **Use paragraph breaks.** They make anything written easier to read.
- **Include your name and e-mail address.** They need not go on a separate line, however. Many people dispense with a closing as well, although it's smoother and friendlier to add a traditional business closing, such as "Regards" or "Sincerely," before signing your name.
- **Don't use a silly moniker for business e-mail.** They are unprofessional, and you'll only look foolish.

Question & Answer

Q: I've always been overweight and only recently lost enough weight to make me happy. So, when I recently got e-mail at work, I decided my online tag would be Tiny. I was surprised when I came in to work one day and found out that my boss was enraged to discover this. Did I do something all that bad?

A: Maybe. Your boss may have overreacted for reasons of his own (what does he weigh?), but you still should not have used a nickname—let alone a cute one—to conduct business. You are representing your company, even when you're online. Any name but your own is simply not appropriate. It also may be misleading to potential customers.

Answering E-mail

It is possible to reply to an e-mail by writing a message at the bottom of the transmittal, but this isn't always a smart thing to do. Software permits this, but not everyone knows about it, and the person on the receiving end may simply think the e-mail didn't go through. Also, writing a reply on someone else's e-mail is sort of like writing a response on the bottom of a snail-mail letter and sending it back.

Neither of these practices is a major offense, but both are a little lacking in polish.

It's Not Private

Another very important thing to keep in mind when using e-mail is that, contrary to popular belief, it is not at all private in the workplace. E-mail is often saved to a special file, and many companies review their workers' e-mail on a regular basis on the grounds that this is just like reading any other business communication that their employees generate.

Therefore, e-mail is not the place to sound off about how much you hate the boss or how silly a coworker (or a customer) is. Nor is it the place to gossip, joke, or describe details of your or anyone else's private life.

Many employers rightfully suspect that workers indulge in e-mail when they should be doing their jobs. So, it also behooves you not to write anything or to send e-mail in such quantities that your employer is able to discover that you are wasting company time.

ONLINE MANNERS

Apart from e-mail, there are several important, rapidly expanding business uses of online services, including the World Wide Web. One can locate, buy, and sell products and services; locate new and used equipment; conduct a job search; or do work-related research online.

It's important to make sure your company is well represented online, just as it is when you use other forms of communication. This means, first of all, being courteous on those occasions when you have human interactions. If someone asks you for help or service, respond as quickly as you can. Electronic communications are nothing if not immediate, and customers want a ready response.

When you ask for help or otherwise use an online service, be polite to the people you come in contact with, too. If someone helps you, online etiquette ("netiquette") does not demand that you send a thank-you note unless you have regular, ongoing contact with that person. Most Web communications are brief and to the point.

And Remember...

- Use the same degree of courtesy with high-tech communications that you use with the older technologies.
- Apologize when a new technology, such as a speaker phone or a cellular phone, puts someone else at a disadvantage.
- Don't become slack about form when using the new technologies. If you're sending a message via e-mail, make it as formal as any other business communication.
- Be sure the new office technology speeds up your work and makes it more efficient, not the other way around.

CHAPTER | 6

HOW TO BE A TEAM PLAYER

In most offices, people have to work closely together. Getting along well with others and getting others to work well together are important job skills that come naturally to some people, less naturally to others—but anyone can learn how. In this chapter, you will learn how to foster a work environment in which everyone does his or her job effectively.

The most important rule for getting along with others at work is this: Be a team player. Office life is communal, and any place of business, whether it is an office or a factory, tends to operate like a small community.

Most offices are made up of either formal or informal teams of people who work together. In some offices, the teams take shape informally; in others, people are assigned to teams. However you land on a team, there probably will be some people on it you like, and some people you don't. The reverse is often true, too: Some people will like you, and some won't. With some sensitivity and a good grounding in office protocol, though, you should be able to get along with everyone at least well enough to work together.

BUILDING ALLIANCES

One of the most important tasks of a team player is to build alliances. In a sense, these are friendships, but work friendships are not always the same as social ones. In an office, you are more likely to befriend people with whom you must work closely as well as those who have special expertise that can help you do your job. They may or may not also be your close personal friends on a social level.

Alliances don't build themselves. To make any alliance or team work for you, you must invest some effort:

- **Be equally nice to (almost) everyone.** The only people you should keep some distance from are the problem personalities, who never quite get the hang of teamwork.
- **Offer to help others when they need it.** The best way to convince someone to help you is to have helped them first.
- **Seek out the people who get things done.** Shamelessly cozy up to the best or most experienced workers, because they are the ones who accomplish the work and, ultimately, will impress the boss.

When Rivalry Rears Its Ugly Head

No matter how hard you try to build alliances with some people, a few will refuse to be brought on board. Some people seem to be more comfortable as rivals than as team players. They won't work with you because they think the best way for them to get ahead is to work against you. What they don't realize is that it is possible to be a team player, even to work closely with someone, and still recognize that person as a rival. Two people vying for the same promotion or for the boss's attention are rivals, but being so doesn't have to mean that they can't work together.

A healthy, open rivalry can encourage you both to do a better job. The only dangerous rivals are the ones who insist on only knocking down your efforts or standing by to watch you rise or fall. These rivals need special handling. Unfortunately, most offices have one or two of these.

Handling the Minor-League Bad Guys

Every office has its roster of small-time bad guys—time wasters, rebels, sabotagers, gossips, and general malcontents. These people will spoil a job for you from the very first day if you let them. A few will seriously undermine you once they see

---

Guidelines: Being Gracious to Rivals

The best way to feel better when someone else gets the promotion you thought should have been yours is to do something nice for that person. To look good when you are feeling low, try these tactics:

- **Offer your congratulations immediately.** Don't wait around—the votes will not be recounted.
- **Keep the attention on the other person.** This is not the time to discuss your equal talents, talk about why you weren't promoted, or let someone cozy up to you and whisper that it should have been yours. Deflect all such comments, for the time being at least.
- **Buy a congratulatory card for the person who was promoted.** Then, have everyone in the office sign it.
- **Give a small gift.** An offering of goodwill says volumes, and you'll feel good about yourself, too.
- **Organize a celebration.** Bring doughnuts or buy a round of drinks.
- **Invite out your rival.** Make it a celebratory lunch or after-work drinks.

---

that you are not going to join the ranks of the disgruntled (i.e., that you prefer to be a team player).

Hanging out with these characters even briefly can make you look bad. No boss wants to look out his or her office door and see employees obviously gossiping with another, or so engrossed in their tête-à-tête that it looks like they're planning a mutiny.

Because bad guys don't like anyone or anything, they can give you a false view of the workplace and even of your job. It's up to you not to let this happen.

Handling bad guys takes some finesse, but it can be done. Here's how:

- **Politely keep your distance.** Don't be rude; just be cool and slightly vague.
- **Don't be seen huddling with them.** Bosses look, see, and record impressions. These impressions can come back to haunt you later.
- **Don't join forces.** Specifically, don't sign their memos or attend any secret meetings they organize.
- **Be patient.** Management has a way of weeding out the troublemakers.

Handling the Major-League Bad Guys

The major-league bad guys are trickier to deal with, but they must be handled. Ignoring someone who is truly subverting your job can be damaging to your career and your reputation.

These bad guys seem to fall into three general types. Each requires a different strategy.

The Credit Stealer

This person wants credit for everything, including what you've done. The best way to deal with a credit stealer is directly. Say, "I am not going to allow you to take credit for work I have done." Then, do whatever you have to do to keep your work out of sight of prying eyes. Put your suggestions in writing, but don't ask this person to read memos before you circulate them and don't discuss your ideas or plans where stealing ears can hear.

The best thing you can do is circulate an idea before the credit stealer does, but if this person continually steals your ideas, let your boss know. Try to do it casually and positively but do make the point that you had the idea first or have a better idea.

The Betrayer

This person wins your trust only to stab you in the back. The betrayer is easily spotted by experienced office workers—not so easily by the inexperienced. He or she usually woos the victim over lunch or an after-work drink to collect the information needed to do the damage. Then, at the first opportunity, the betrayer turns everything you've said in confidence against you, laying out all your insecurities and fears to your boss.

Discretion is the best way to cope with a betrayer. Don't talk too much or too openly when he or she is around, and certainly don't share your fears and anxieties. In other words, don't give the betrayer any ammunition.

It also is helpful to maintain your own direct pipeline to your boss. Never let the betrayer deliver any information on your behalf.

The Underminer

This person does the damage to your face. The underminer's goal is to make you feel worthless and incompetent, exactly how he or she feels.

The best strategy against the underminer is avoidance. Don't let this person into your conversation. Politely cut off the underminer when he or she says things you don't like. There's no real way to help this person, who needs help him- or herself, so it's best to steer clear.

🔍 CASE HISTORY

Elaine took credit for all Betsy's work and stole her ideas, even though she and Betsy were confidantes and worked closely together. Time and again, Betsy would be working on a memo filled with ideas to present to the boss only to discover that Elaine had beaten her to the punch.

Betsy wasn't sure how this happened repeatedly, but she set out to correct the situation. Initially, she had confided in Elaine, but after the first problem, she stopped doing that. Betsy began to lock her file cabinet at night and even started locking her office door.

Betsy suspected that someone had access to her computer files, but she couldn't prove it. One morning, she noticed that a computer file she was about to work on had been used around 7 p.m. the night before, long after she had left the office. Betsy realized that Elaine probably tapped into her computer and read her files after she left work.

Betsy escalated her measures. She started using a password that closed to her files to everyone. When she finished her next memo, she quietly sent it off to her boss without saying a word about it to Elaine.

For the first time in months, Betsy's idea got to the boss first, and she got the credit she deserved. Elaine was forced to stop her rivalrous antics when she realized Betsy was on to her.

Handling Your Own Rivalrous Feelings

It is a good idea to make sure that you are a good rival yourself. To do this, you may have to reorient your thinking. In school, rivals typically were athletic opponents—other team members you saw once or twice a year for the sole purpose of emerging victorious over them.

At work, though, rivals are people you see every day, work closely with, and must at least give the appearance of getting along with. If you can't work well with someone for any reason, you'll only diminish your own chances of getting ahead.

Keeping Your Competitiveness in Check

Here are some hints for keeping your own competitiveness in check as well as disarming others:

- **Develop a "may-the-best-person-win" attitude, at least publicly.** Secretly, you may be unhappy that all your hard work hasn't paid off with a promotion or some other reward, but never let this show. Instead, take the more professional attitude that you win some, and the other guy wins some. Maybe you both get promoted; if only one of you can be promoted, then there will be another chance for the person who doesn't win this time.
- **Avoid dirty tactics.** For one thing, it is really hard to pull them off without others seeing what you are up to and, consequently, thinking less of you. Most bosses know who plays fair and who doesn't, so it is in your best long-term interests to play fair.
- **Confront a rival who constantly uses nasty tactics against you.** The most common ones are undermining your work or taking credit for it. When this happens, try to arrange a private meeting. Tell the person you know what they have done and that you do not like it. A rival who is forewarned has to be far more careful than one who thinks he or she hasn't been discovered yet.
- **Stay civil, even if open warfare has broken out.** Some people don't know how to do this, but you'll look good if you can manage it.
- **Keep the dispute private.** Even if a rival undermines you in front of others, smile as you insist, "Let's discuss this later."
- **Never wilt in front of a rival.** That's exactly what he or she hopes will happen. Go right ahead and make your points, even if you have to interrupt your rival to do so. Some people count on taking over a meeting with the force of their personality, but you don't have to let this happen.
- **Never show your anger.** If you keep cool while your rival busily runs circles around you, you're likely to make that person angry. Whoever gets angry first usually looks bad or weak.

When Everyone Is Disgruntled

If you have somehow managed to land in an office or a department where everyone seems to be unhappy or overly rivalrous—even management—then you may have a bigger problem on your hands. It is possible that this simply is not a well-run company, and you may want to think about moving on.

DEALING WITH THE OFFICE GRAPEVINE

Another element of office life that undermines team play is the office grapevine. Every office seems to have one, along with one person who fuels it. The only issue for you is how to handle the various situations it can present. Your goal should be neither to contribute to it nor to be a topic on it. To accomplish this goal, follow these rules:

- **Hesitate to talk much about your private life at work.** Wait for questions. Don't make announcements. Provide few details when asked.
- **Don't repeat what you have heard, true or not.** It's not fun to be in the middle of a divorce so devastating you can barely drag yourself to work each morning. Never add to a person's woes by talking about them behind someone's back.
- **Don't gossip to the boss.** Bosses don't mind gossips, because they are their pipeline to what's going on in the office. Sooner or later, if you're the office snitch, the boss will wonder what you're saying about him or her.

TALKING TO THE BOSS ABOUT TROUBLEMAKERS

As a last resort, you may have to talk to your boss about an office troublemaker. Do this only after you have tried to work it out with the individual, and be sure to let the boss know you tried to handle the situation on your own first.

Couch whatever you say in as positive a fashion as you can. Don't simply say, "John has been taking credit for my work." Instead, say, "John is a very hard worker, and although he has some good ideas, I find that he also borrows other people's ideas." A smart boss will know what you're saying or ask for more facts so he or she can figure out what's going on.

GETTING THE GOOD GUYS TO LEND A HAND

Fortunately, despite the few villains, most offices are populated with well-balanced, helpful, pleasant people that you will be happy to have on your team.

It is always wiser to cultivate friendships with these people than to waste time with the bad guys. In fact, once you know them well enough, they can help you by filling you in on the villains' history and offering suggestions on how to work around them.

Guidelines: Complaining

It's always tricky to complain about a fellow worker, but sometimes it's unavoidable. Still, there is a right—and a wrong—way to do it. Here are some ideas:

- **Always speak to the person before talking to management.** Then, make sure the boss knows you did this.
- **Enlist other people's support.** Do this, even if only to confirm that you are not the only one who finds a person troublesome. There is strength in numbers. If possible, get others to go with you when you talk to the boss about the problem.
- **Drop hints before using a direct approach.** Say to your boss, "We had some unusual problems completing this report," then hope he or she takes the bait and asks what they were.
- **Couch your complaint in positive language.** Instead of complaining, "Tim never delivers anything on time," explain, "Tim is basically a good worker, but he tended to deliver late on this project, and that hurt all of us."
- **Don't make it personal.** Describe the situation, and express your concern. Never sound as if you're whining. If you're good, it won't even sound like you're complaining!

Also helpful is to always keep your own line of communication to your boss open. Make it a practice to occasionally drop by your boss's office to chat at the end of the day. Let him or her know you have opinions and are willing to share them. Make sure your boss sees all the memos you write, even those not addressed to him or her.

OFFICE FRIENDSHIPS

One of the perks of working in an office is the friends you make. Personal friendships need to be handled a carefully, though. You won't want your group of friends to become such a tight little knot, or clique, that others are excluded. When you and your friends form your own inner circle, you risk having people think you don't really belong to the big team any longer—and this is never good.

Even if you have a special friend, always try to include other workers in at least some of your conversations and activities. When you go to lunch or for happy hour, for example, occasionally ask others to join you. Don't share "in" jokes or make comments that others don't understand. As much as possible, try to be inclusive—at least while you are at work.

DAILY LIFE IN AND AROUND THE OFFICE

Aside from dealing with personalities, all workers need to learn how to get along on a daily basis at work. Even among otherwise congenial colleagues, small spats and disagreements occasionally pop up and must be resolved. Interestingly, the vast majority of complaints about coworkers revolve around two topics: food and tobacco.

Food

It is okay to eat at work, provided you do so in a way that is not offensive to those around you. You should follow a few specific guidelines:

- **Try to eat only at mealtime.** An office is not a smorgasbord, and the fact that you can eat at your desk is not a license to eat there all day long. Your coworkers will find the smells tempting, annoying, or simply too strong. You'll also look as if you're not doing your job.
- **Make sure it is permitted.** Before you ever eat at your desk, check the rules. A few companies don't allow it.
- **Clean up immediately after you eat.** A desk littered with half-eaten food is seriously unattractive to everyone who passes by.
- **Never store unwrapped or perishable food in your desk.** The food will smell, insects and rodents will love it, and people will hate it—and possibly you as well.
- **Skip the diet talk.** This is one of the world's most boring subjects anyway, but one that often monopolizes office chitchat. If you are dieting, keep it mostly to yourself, then enjoy the pleasant moment when your coworkers first notice.
- **Don't tempt dieters.** Even when diets aren't a staple of office talk, everyone knows who is on one—and who isn't. Don't torture those who are by offering temptation in the form of candy bars, chocolates, or anything else that isn't on their diets.

Smoking

It is hard to find a more politically incorrect activity, inside or outside the office, than smoking.

Many workplaces have banned smoking in the building, and some states have done so. None of this has stopped smokers from smoking, however, so your best bet is to cause as little annoyance as possible if you must smoke. Here are some ways you can do this:

- **Smoke only in designated areas.** Do not smoke in areas that are unsafe, such as stairwells and restrooms.
- **If you can smoke at your desk, do so discreetly.** No one should have to breathe your second-hand smoke all day. If you chain-smoke, don't do it at your desk. Step outside at least part of the time.
- **Cooperate when someone asks you not to smoke—even if the request seems unfair.** The world is against you on this one, and it's better not to make trouble. Besides, many people do have allergies that make it impossible for them to be around smoke.
- **Think about quitting.** Research shows that bosses think smokers are messier, less efficient, and less attentive than nonsmokers.

Other Annoying Habits

Humans are capable of developing any number of annoying minor habits that can drive others crazy, especially when they work closely together day after day. One way to be liked is to be aware of what these are and to try to rein them in. For example, please don't

- whistle,
- whisper,
- speak loudly,
- clip your fingernails,
- crack your knuckles,
- crack gum or chew it loudly, or
- tap on your desk or keyboard.

On the other hand, don't worry about a habit you can't do much about, such as a nervous cough or sighing.

Office Humor

Like all close-knit communities, offices tend to develop their own "in" jokes and special brand of humor. These are fine, as long as they don't get out of hand and aren't directed at individuals.

It's okay to join in a few pranks, but it is not smart to become known as the office jokester, lest your boss think you don't take work seriously. The office prankster is usually viewed by management as something of a buffoon.

Also, try to keep sarcasm to a minimum, even if it is your natural style. Your friends outside work may understand your dry sense of humor because they know and love you, but at work, it is too easily misunderstood. You run the risk of being labeled a bitter, angry person.

THE PAYOFF

Teamwork usually leads toward several goals. One, of course, is to get the job done well. Another is to get promoted. The irony about getting promoted, though, is that it often breaks up the team or at least temporarily upsets the camaraderie.

Therefore, part of being a good team player is knowing how to handle the situation when you are promoted, as well as when you are not.

When You Are Promoted

When your big day arrives, do everything you can to handle it with grace:

- **Don't leak your promotion in advance, even to your closest friends.** This way, you can act somewhat surprised and modest when it happens.
- **Be modest when accepting congratulations.** Simply say thank you. There's no need to reiterate what clever action you took that earned you this promotion.
- **Be sure to thank your team.** To be honest, most promotions should be shared with any number of people. Be generous about sharing yours. Make this is a team victory, and people will love you for it.

When You're Not Promoted

The best way to handle other people's promotions is to enjoy them. Try to keep a sense of proportion about them. If today wasn't your day, then perhaps tomorrow will be. In the meantime, do everything you can to be happy for the person who was promoted.

When someone else wins the reward you were hoping for, try to be the first person to step up and offer congratulations.

CASE HISTORY

Sally knew that Bill needed to get a presentation ready for their boss by 9 a.m. Tuesday morning, and it was now Monday at 4 p.m. Bill had printed out the main report and still needed to collate all the materials into one package.

When Bill mentioned to Sally that he would have to miss his child's school play in order to get this done, Sally volunteered to stay and do it. This meant Sally had to cancel her plans, but she quickly sized up her plans as being less important to her than Bill's were to him. Sally also counted on—correctly, as it turned out—Bill's help the next time she was in a crunch with work.

The moral of this story is this: Workplace favors count, and they get repaid. One of the best ways to build solid alliances to others is to help them out when they need it most.

And Remember ...

- Be a team player.
- Build careful alliances.
- Rivals are team members, too.
- Play office politics when you must, but play fairly.
- Keep annoying habits to a minimum.
- Be kind to everyone but slow to cultivate friendships.

CHAPTER | 7

WORKING WITH CUSTOMERS

There's a line from an old mining song that goes, "I owe my soul to the company store." These days, though, the situation is often reversed. As more companies sell services instead of products, they owe everything to their employees—especially those who work directly with customers.

The employees who work with customers in many ways *are* the company. They are its personality. They bring it to life, and they are responsible for much of the company's profits. If you work with customers or clients, you should know how to treat them—and how to keep them coming back.

WHAT THE COMPANY EXPECTS

On the Large Scale

Employers look for certain social traits when hiring sales or service people. The three major ones are loyalty, confidence, and discretion.

Loyalty

Loyalty, despite being not much admired these days, is nevertheless an important trait in an employee who works in sales or service. Your employer anticipates that you will positively promote the company's products and services. Additionally, it is expected that you will stand by the overall philosophy of the company, including its approach to sales.

Confidence

Companies also expect their sales and service personnel to project confidence in its products, its services, and its image. Undermining them would be a serious offense.

Discretion

All companies have some information they want kept private: internal turmoil, new products in the pipeline, and attempts to resolve philosophical issues, for example. As an employee who has contact with customers, it is up to you to be discreet about the information you share with them.

Guidelines: The Right Attitude

In working with customers, attitude is everything. Therefore, it is important that you do two things when you represent your company to customers:

- **Be proud.** If you aren't truly proud of your company and your place in it, you will find it hard to represent them. If you are, you will find it easy to tout your company's products and services.
- **Be positive.** Whereas you may find it an effective sales tool to point out a weakness in a product or service that will be of special interest to a client, always couch it in strengths, and present both in the most positive light.

On the Small Scale

In addition to the major social traits, companies want salespeople who can exercise a degree of skill, or social finesse, in their dealings with customers. In a sense, customers are guests at a company's banquet, and the salespeople are the hosts.

Meeting and Greeting

Customers should be made to feel like special people. How you treat your customers has a real effect on where they choose to do their business. To make your company the one your customers want to do business with, try to do these four things:

- **Be happy.** Always try to sound and look happy to see or hear from a customer.
- **Be gracious.** Tell the receptionist to let you know immediately when a customer arrives, and then walk out to greet him or her. This is truly gracious behavior.
- **Be helpful.** Alternately, ask the receptionist to deliver the customers to your office if possible, instead of leaving them to find their own way.
- **Be welcoming.** As the "host," stand and extend your hand in greeting.

Introductions

Whenever it is appropriate to do so, introduce the customer to your coworkers. The more people the customer meets who work for the company, the more chances he or she has to be impressed. So, make a point of introducing a visiting customer to everyone you can, especially to anyone who will work with him or her.

You even may want to plan some of the introductions. Be sure to inform coworkers when a customer will be visiting, and make plans for them to drop by your office or meeting room. Alternately, you can take the customer around to the employees' offices.

If you want to introduce the boss—and customers always like this—it's smart to arrange this meeting in advance. By the way, this is a win-win situation. In addition to impressing the customer, you'll also impress the boss when you ask whether you can drop by with a special customer.

When making introductions, present your fellow worker to the customer, not the other way around. Keep the presentation simple. You might say, "Joy, I'd like you to meet Juan Navarro. He works in public relations and has been assigned to handle your account." Juan should not need to be told who Joy is; he should know that she is the first vice president of the new banking account you just got. In fact, one reason to let your fellow workers know that they will be meeting a customer is so they will be up-to-date on the project and have something interesting to say about it.

Probably the only time you'll introduce a colleague to a customer is when the only two people in the company conceivably rank higher than the customer (e.g., the president of the company or the chairman of the board). Even then, if the customer if important enough, then it may be appropriate to introduce the president and CEO, not the other way around.

Guidelines: Making Introductions

Introductions can be tricky if you don't know the rules. A good general rule of thumb to follow when making them is to introduce lower-ranking persons to higher-ranking ones:

- **Introduce young people to older people.**
- **Introduce men to women.** It may be old fashioned, but it's still accepted protocol.
- **Introduce subordinates to superiors.** This usually takes precedence over the previous two guidelines. For example, a new employee, even an elderly woman, would be introduced to her male boss, not the other way around. And an older employee would be introduced to a younger boss.
- **Introduce coworkers to public officials.** Your coworkers also include your boss and other superiors.
- **Introduce everyone to clergy.**

Even with these helpful guidelines, sometimes you simply have to make a judgment call—for example, when you are introducing the president of your company and the mayor.

MEETING IN THE CUSTOMER'S OFFICE

Most of the time, you will meet customers on their home turf, so you will need to know how to set up and conduct this kind of meeting.

First, when you call a customer to request a meeting, begin by asking whether it is a convenient time, either to talk or to meet. If the time is good, mention why you want the meeting ("to show you our new line," "to smooth out the details of your project," "to introduce the new junior account executive"). Most customers also find it helpful if you indicate how much time you will need for the meeting.

On the day of your meeting, you should keep a few points in mind:

- **Dress up a little.** Especially if you are making a sales pitch, the customer will be impressed that the presentation matters enough for you to put on your best pin-striped suit. People sense these things. They don't have to know that you ordinarily wear jeans to work to appreciate that your wearing the pin-striped suit is a compliment.

- **Bring everything with you that you need.** If you need a podium or an easel for a presentation, be sure to bring it. If you need audiovisual equipment or a computer, think about scheduling the meeting on your premises, if possible, where you will be using your equipment that you are totally familiar with.

- **Arrive on time.** Customers are too important to keep waiting. You, however, aren't subject to the same rules—at least not on this occasion. So, if a client asks you to wait 10 minutes or even 30, graciously agree.

- **Accept coffee, tea, or food if it's offered.** Just remember that you won't look very slick if you're stuffing your mouth while trying to talk.

- **Request a beverage before you start.** Nervousness and public speaking can make your throat scratchy, so get a glass of water or a cup of tea before you begin. It's better than interrupting your presentation midstream and losing the attention of your audience or your train of thought.

- **You may want to decline alcoholic beverages.** There is no hard-and-fast rule, but when you are about to make a presentation, it may be smart to keep your beverage consumption to a minimum. Alcohol and beverages with caffeine especially can make you start to feel antsy after a few minutes, before you even hit the high points of your presentation.

- **Don't overstay your welcome.** Unless something major is undecided regarding the project, most meetings wear a little thin after an hour or so.

MEETING IN YOUR OFFICE

Customers will sometimes come to your office to meet. When you invite a customer, be sure to explain why—you want to give a tour of the facilities or you need some equipment to make a presentation that otherwise you would have made at the customer's office.

In addition, a few more logistics need to be tended to:

- **Arrange for transportation if necessary.** It is a good idea when you work in a place that is difficult to find or to get to. At minimum, offer directions.

- **Decide in advance where you are going to meet.** Your office is fine, provided it is large and pleasant and clean enough. When you have a prearranged meeting with a customer, it is a given that you will clean house first. You can get away with disarray when you are faced with a last-minute or unexpected visit, but not when the visit has been scheduled in advance. Boardrooms are another good place to meet because they are usually both impressive and expansive.

- **Look good.** It will be even more flattering to your customer if other employees are casually dressed. He or she will realize that you made an extra effort for this occasion.

- **Make sure everything is ready.** Seating, props, charts, transparencies, and beverages should be ready before your customer arrives. It is tempting to let things go until the last minute when you're on your home turf, but don't risk it. You want everything to go as well as it would were you to give the presentation at the customer's place of business.

- **Offer all attendees a beverage.** During regular work hours, offer a nonalcoholic drink, but after work hours, alcoholic beverages might be more appropriate. Whether you do this or not depends on what is customary in your business and at your company.

- **Arrange to have your calls held.** This is a smart and flattering thing to do for a casual meeting as well as for a major presentation.

- **Provide food if the meeting will be long or extend into mealtime.** Plan the food in advance and order something delicious, even impressively so. You needn't order a multi-course meal, but if you're serving sandwiches, for example, then get some gourmet ones, not the run-of-the-mill ones offered in the company cafeteria. If you will be taking individual food orders, do it before you start your presentation, and take a break to eat it when it arrives. Eating and listening can be a mutually exclusive activity in which the eating often wins out.

- **Keep the meeting to a reasonable length.** This rule is no different from when you meet at a client's office. You may be eager to show off everything, but you will not want your customer to feel like a captive.

ASSERTIVELY POLITE SELLING

Whether during a presentation or in the daily course of your work, all or part of your job may be to sell either a product or a service. Whereas there is a definite technique to selling—which can be learned in a class or seminar or even from books—only rarely is the protocol of selling explained in these classes. So, here are some tips that will help to set the tone for your salesmanship:

CASE HISTORY

One of Jennifer's most important customers made passes at her constantly. She had to travel to his city two or three times a month to service the account, and he invariably tried to get her to schedule their meeting for the end of the day. Then, he would insist that they have drinks, usually at her hotel, and often dropped hints about going to her room. She turned him down but eventually felt her refusals were not enough. She wanted to settle the issue so that he would stop asking—and she hopefully would still have a customer.

Jennifer scheduled a late-morning appointment and then invited her customer to lunch. When he made his usual advance, she tactfully managed to both flatter him and tell him no, once and for all. She accomplished this by saying that although she found him attractive, she had a firm policy never to date customers. She added that her company disapproved, and any involvement with a customer could get her in trouble or even cost her job.

This direct approach worked, and Jennifer never had a another problem. She also never scheduled another late-afternoon appointment.

- **Thank the person for seeing you.** Keep this brief, however, because there's nothing worse that starting a sales call with blatant fawning.
- **Take a few minutes to make small talk.** Watch carefully to make sure you don't overdo it, but it is always a good idea to set the mood with a little social chitchat. By the way, this is one time when it is perfectly appropriate to discuss otherwise boring subjects like the weather, public transportation, or how long your commute was this morning.
- **Don't get personal.** Even if it would help you to know whether a potential customer is married or divorced, childless or a parent, don't ask now. There will be time later to get to know each other a little better, but it is too calculating and obvious to tie such questions to a sales call—especially when it later becomes obvious that you are going to use this information in your sales pitch.
- **Honest flattery is the best policy.** Only keep it to a minimum. Most people are a little wary during a sales call anyway (perhaps they know that you are there to manipulate them), so believe it or not, flattery is not always well-received.
- **Thank the person again when you leave.** Again, keep it short. Say that you appreciate his or her giving you the time to make the presentation. Don't

linger after you have said what you came to say. Leave while you can still leave behind a good impression.

- **Be sure to follow up.** Send along any materials you said you would, along with a gracious note saying how appreciative you were of the chance to meet. If no follow-up is necessary, it is still gracious to send a brief thank-you note.

- **Call back when you say you will.** If you say you will call back in two weeks, then do it. Doing what you say will show that you are trustworthy and build your customer's confidence in you.

❓ Question & Answer

Q: My compliments to customers seem to fall flat. I mean them, but I don't think I sound truly sincere. What can I do?

A: Flattery is a delicate art, never more so than when dealing with customers. Sometimes when we are courting someone, we try to get close to them through flattery, even if the compliments aren't always honest.

Resolve right now to make only honest compliments to customers. Keep them specific, too. Don't call someone "wonderful." Instead, say that you admire his or her energy or that you think the way he or she reorganized the department is really great. Make your compliments brief—people get embarrassed when someone goes on and on even in a nice way. But do give compliments! A few well-intended honest words of praise can make someone's day.

Cold Calls

These are sales calls you make when you don't know the person you are calling. Often, new employees who work in sales are expected to generate business through this method. There is a right and a wrong way to go about making a cold call:

- **Identify yourself.** Say hello warmly, then clearly state your name and that of your company.

- **State your purpose immediately.** People rightfully become annoyed when they do not immediately know that they are listening to a sales call.

- **Take a hint.** If the person clearly indicates no interest, end the call as politely as it started.

- **Be accommodating.** If the caller is interested in talking with you but says this is a bad time, offer to call back. If you sense the person has the time, solicit a better time to call. If the person appears to be too busy for even this, then end the call as quickly as you can and take your chances when you call again.

- **Keep your word.** Call back when you say you will, to the day, if possible.

- **Be polite.** Even if the person puts you on hold, asks you to wait, and isn't particularly warm to you, you don't have to act that way, too.

- **Bow out graciously.** Say good-bye politely, even if the results are not what you hoped for. Try not to express your anger at poor or cold treatment (this is a cold call, after all). Remember that you never know when you will meet again—under other circumstances.

WARM, FUZZY FEELINGS

It is not uncommon, especially among inexperienced workers, to develop friendly feelings toward customers and clients. After all, you spend a great deal of your time courting them and getting to know them, perhaps even entertaining them outside work. It is only natural that you might become friends. Right? Well, wrong—or at least not very wise.

Consider this scenario. For as long as you work for XYZ Company, your loyalties are to them, not to the customer whom you are thinking could become your new best friend. Unfortunately, this situation puts a damper on any real friendship. After all, there will be information you will not be able to share because of your loyalty to your company that your customer, in turn, may expect you to share because of your friendship. You have created a clear conflict of interest. Similarly, you will feel pain if your customer, who has now become your dear friend, announces that he or she will now be doing business with someone else.

For these and other reasons, it is difficult to become friends with clients and maintain the professional distance you need to work with them and still be loyal to your company. Therefore, the best thing you can do, for yourself, your company, and your customers, is to maintain a friendly but definitely professional distance.

And Remember ...

- Loyalty and confidence are two of the most important qualities that employers seek in workers who deal with customers.
- Be discreet about sharing company business, especially problems, with customers.
- You are the "host" to a customer any time you are together.
- Advance preparation is one of the best things you can do to make all customer contacts go smoothly.
- Maintain a friendly but professional relationship with your customers.

CHAPTER | 8

WHEN YOU'RE IN CHARGE

Even if you are not a manager, there may be occasions when you will find yourself supervising the work of others. You may oversee the work of summer interns or temporary workers, give assignments to the typing pool, or have an assistant, for example. You may even find yourself supervising people you once worked with.

A supervisory position is usually easier to accept when you are formally promoted to another job. However, more often, you will find yourself informally supervising a colleague. This situation can be far more difficult to handle.

SUPERVISING WITH STYLE

Successful managers know that supervision involves getting people to do what you want them to do—and letting them think it was their idea in the first place. The best managers use a light hand; they don't hold it over people that they're in charge, and they don't make people do unnecessary work or follow a bunch of silly rules. Their only goal is to get the work done as efficiently as possible.

Tact Is the Key

American workers are very independent. They like to think that they answer to no one, and given the slightest reason to resist—a young or inexperienced supervisor, for example—they will. Therefore, tact is a very necessary ingredient for the new or temporary manager dealing with subordinates.

There are many ways to be tactful to someone who works for you:

- **Use praise to motivate.** Don't try to fake it—people are quick to spot the phony variety. They do respond to honest compliments, though.
- **Criticize in private.** Some people find it humiliating to be criticized by someone young, inexperienced, or not officially their boss. Offering criticism behind closed doors is a good way to avoid this problem.
- **Set a good example.** Nothing is more galling than a new manager who tells others what to do while failing to pull his or her own weight. If others see that you work as hard as they do, you will find you have crossed a big hurdle in getting them to work hard for you.
- **Give commands in the form of questions.** These are softer and easier to accept. For example, instead of ordering, "I need this letter by noon," try asking, "Do you think you could possibly get this letter done for me by noon?" This should inspire your subordinate to rise to your gentle challenge.
- **Soften all your language.** Rather than issuing commands, suggest, "You may want to do it this way" or "Have you thought about this approach?"
- **Take subordinates into your confidence when you can.** Only high-powered executives can issue orders without any explanation. The rest of us fare better if we offer a reason, for example, "The chairman needs this letter for a report he's submitting to the board this afternoon. Do you think you could possibly get this letter done for me by then?"

Don't Talk Too Much

Taking subordinates into your confidence doesn't mean that you have to share your every thought or confidential company information with them. Your goal is to tell people enough to motivate them.

Talking too much is a common mistake of new and inexperienced managers. It reveals your insecurity about not having a lot of experience, gives people ammunition to use against you if they don't want to take orders from you, and gives the office bad guys—the ones who don't want you to succeed—ammunition to use in undermining you.

Tell people enough that they are encouraged to do the job well, and then close your mouth.

THE RIGHT PROTOCOL

Jan, who just became the first female floor manager in the superstore where she works, is having trouble with Susie, one of her workers. Because they have known each other and worked together for many years, Jan has invited Susie to lunch so they can talk.

Jan can tell that Susie doesn't like working for her. Jan thinks that this is not because they used to work together but because Susie is uncomfortable working for a woman. She is sure that Susie is as surprised as anyone to find out that she resents having a woman for a boss.

Jan feels she should seize the initiative and bring up the subject in a direct way, but should she?

As boss, Jan does have the right to take the initiative, but this may not be the best way to handle this particular situation. People often respond badly when they are told what is wrong with them.

Jan might do better to talk about how it feels to be the first woman in this position—and how it must feel strange as well to those who work for her. This opens the door for Susie to recognize her own problem. This, in turn, should lead to honest discussion of the problem.

Bringing out the Big Guns

When gentle prodding fails, you can always force people to do their jobs. After all, you probably are requesting something in the name of the person who is superior to both you and your subordinate. If being reminded of this fact will inspire an employee to work, then by all means use it.

This tactic not only is acceptable but also may be helpful. For example, if George repeatedly (and somewhat belligerently) persists in taking two-hour lunches, instead of throwing your weight around, throw around the boss's weight.

Say to George, quite confidentially, "Listen, Mr. Pross noticed that you're taking long lunches. I thought I'd mention it to you quietly before he says anything." You'll make points with your coworker for the tip, and hopefully, the behavior will be curtailed.

When You're Younger

It can be very difficult to be in a position of power over someone who is much older than you are. This calls for some special strategies:

- **Forget the age difference.** This isn't school, where a few years' difference in age mattered. In most workplaces, age really is irrelevant.
- **Avoid references to age.** Maybe you think 50 is old, but people who are 50 feel (and are) pretty young. In fact, you will only be playing up your own youthful inexperience if you constantly remark on how old 40 or 50 is.
- **Don't be overly respectful—at least in a formal way.** Calling an older man "Mr." or "Sir" when you're giving him work may only make him feel older. If you call everyone else by a first name, do so with this person as well.
- **Take time to ask older workers about their experience.** In the process, you might even learn something that will be really helpful to you as you do your job. People like to think experience counts—and they are grateful when they see signs that you agree with them.
- **Ask more experienced or older workers for advice.** Everyone loves to give advice, and it has been known to co-opt the toughest worker.
- **Publicly play up older workers' strengths.** Say, for example, "Virginia, you were here when the last merger took place. What can you recall that will help us with this one?"
- **Learn to recognize and respect hidden clout.** In every workplace, there are people of relatively low rank who have a great deal of power. This may be the big boss's secretary or a clerk in accounting who once discovered a way to save the company millions and who has had the chairman's ear ever since. You must never undermine their respect if you expect them to work with you.

When You're the Same Age

Sometimes the problem is not getting along with older or younger workers but with workers who are exactly your age—and thus perhaps more prone to rivalrous feelings. To handle this kind of situation, keep these hints in mind:

- **Don't mention your age.** Maybe your peers will think you are older than you are and accord you respect because of this.
- **Show a little compassion.** Go out of your way not to lord your superior power over peers who know you're the same age. Imagine how you would feel if the situation were reversed, and act accordingly.
- **Don't get too chummy.** At the same time that you are showing compassion, maintain a little distance. You can't be friends with people who work for you, but you can be friendly.
- **Occasionally let down your hair with your subordinates.** Talk about a movie you saw or mention that you had a fabulous date last weekend. These kinds of comments remind them that you are human, if not very old or wise in their estimation.
- **Talk straight when you have to.** If a subordinate really is not doing his job because of an attitude problem in working with you, take him or her aside for a talk. Say, "You may not like this working arrangement, but this is the way it is. We both have to make the best of it."

CONFIDING IN THE BOSS

Most bosses know there are potential problems with putting someone relatively new or very young in charge. Good managers should be prepared to help the new ones solve the problems that pop up as a result of age or inexperience.

Try To Resolve It First

If you are having personnel problems, as always, try to resolve them yourself before you go to your boss. Your boss will respect the fact that you sought a solution rather than simply running for help at the first sign of trouble.

When you approach your boss, never attribute the problem to your age, inexperience, or newness to the position. Offer a strictly work-related explanation— anything else would play on your weaknesses, which you don't want to do. For example, rather than assuming, "Joan doesn't like working for me because I'm too young," say, "Joan doesn't seem able to complete her assignments on time." Joan may be indignant to hear how you perceive her problem, but she will probably shape up. If you are doing your job well, she won't be able to say that her only complaint is that you are 10 years younger than she is.

CASE HISTORY

Initially, Gerry's promotion to shop manager at a small car parts company was welcomed by his fellow workers. He had risen through the ranks, so the workers saw Gerry as "one of them."

After a few weeks, however, Gerry's subordinates became distant and cold to him. They no longer invited him to join them at the local pub—which was just as well, really, because with his overwhelming responsibilities, Gerry often had to work late. Gerry's fellow workers didn't realize he was still at the office, though. All they knew was that from the moment Gerry got promoted, he no longer was their reliable drinking buddy.

Gerry thought his former pals were jealous over his promotion, and this served to separate them even more. Gerry suffered in silence until finally, someone hinted at the problem.

The next Friday, Gerry made a point of knocking off early and heading down to the pub. In response to jokes about his "managing to mingle with the common folk," Gerry announced that the company was buying everyone a round of drinks. He made a point of explaining that the company owed him a round for all the extra time he had been putting in. It was a tactful way to break the ice, make his point, and make up with his buddies.

After that, Gerry managed to go out with his fellow workers at least once a month. Their old camaraderie, mixed in with some new respect, soon returned.

Someone Who Won't Shape Up

No matter what you do or how tactful you are, this person hates working for you. He or she may resent all authority, not only your power. Or, maybe this person is one of the office "bad guys" who can't get along with any boss.

In this instance, it may make sense to go to your boss sooner rather than later. Most bosses know who the troublemakers are and usually will call a halt to their antics if they interfere with others' ability to work.

When you realize that you are dealing with someone who is not going to change their behavior, you should take that person out of the loop as soon as you can. Don't share reports, memos, correspondence, or ideas with him or her. That information will only be used against you.

Question & Answer

Q: A vicious office gossip, who used to be my friend, is gossiping about my personal life in an attempt to undermine me at work. To make things worse, I was recently promoted and am now his boss. I think he's saying these things because he resents working for me.

My real problem is that there is some truth to what he is saying. He also is recounting an especially painful and embarrassing episode in my life. What can I do to stop this? Should I order him to stop talking about me?

A: Messengers usually love the attention they get, and they can be harder to stop than you might imagine—especially when there is even a grain of truth in what they are saying. So, talking to this person will probably give him more grist for his mill.

If you possibly can, ignore everything he says, and hope that others do the same. At minimum, this approach will make your problem go away sooner than if you make a fuss about it.

DRESS THE PART

When you're managing anyone, one helpful tactic is to dress the part—of the boss, that is.

Clothes can convey authority, and while you don't have to wear ones that makes you look old or frumpy, you may find that you inspire more authority when you wear a suit than when you wear blue jeans.

When you are young or inexperienced, it pays to use everything at your disposal.

GAINING SKILL

Never be too proud to get some outside assistance when you are first learning how to manage people. The art of managing people is rarely inborn, and someone who is young or inexperienced and thrust into a position of authority over others may especially need help.

Countless books have been written on this subject, and there are seminars and classes as well. Ask friends and superiors how they handle certain situations. The management of people is a skill that one can acquire.

Guidelines: Winning Over Employees

Here are some great ways to woo wary subordinates when you are a new boss:

- **Cater to their stomachs.** Buy a pound of a gourmet coffee for the office, or share donuts, cake, or home-baked cookies.
- **Bring in flowers for the office.** Better yet, if someone sends you flowers to congratulate you on your promotion, put them in a public place where everyone can enjoy them.
- **Take them out to lunch individually.** Use this time together to discuss their work and their future.
- **Have lunch with them off the record, too.** Always eating with the other managers makes you look snobbish or stand-offish.
- **Praise their work.** Make a point to give a lot of honest praise, even in front of others.

Don't Get Angry—Motivate

Pitching a fit when you're the boss is not the same as doing it when you're not. Actually, truly mature people don't ever have temper tantrums at work, but we all know exceptions to this rule. Some of the worst perpetrators are pretty powerful people.

Nevertheless, as long as you are still young enough to master new things, learn not to show anger. It frightens people, and it definitely doesn't motivate them—and that is the very thing that a boss is supposed to do.

Confidentiality

One difficulty in being a young or inexperienced manager is that it is hard to maintain the necessary distance from your peers, who often are your friends. One tempting way to bridge the gap is to share information with others that you ought to keep to yourself. Even older workers who want to cozy up to subordinates sometimes indulge in this bad practice.

Yet, the higher up the ladder you climb, the more privy you will be to confidential information. At any level, leaking information is something your boss will hold against you. Therefore, it is imperative that you learn to keep your mouth closed when necessary. Learning this skill is a prerequisite to your becoming a better manager.

The easiest way to keep confidential information to yourself is not to admit what you know in the first place. When you have told a coworker that you know a corporate secret, it is a small but slippery slope to the next step, which is to begin spilling the confidential beans! If you would not like to find yourself in this position, then train yourself to be silent about matters better left unsaid.

This does not mean you have to clam up totally. Your fellow workers will enjoy hearing what you can share with them, especially good news or amusing anecdotes. Just learn to share only the information that isn't top secret.

And Remember ...

- Tact and sensitivity are required to supervise anyone, but especially people who are much older than or the same age as you.
- Offer praise in public—and in private. Be generous with it!
- Offer criticism privately and tactfully whenever possible.
- Seek out the advice of older or more experienced workers.

CHAPTER | 9

SEX AND OTHER DILEMMAS OF OFFICE LIFE

Not too many years ago, very few women worked, and those who did rarely held positions of power. This fact alone made male-female work relationships fairly simple, if not straightforward.

As growing numbers of women entered the workplace—often in positions of authority—relationships between male and female coworkers have grown more complicated, and new rules have evolved to guide them. Most of these rules pertain to issues such as sexual harassment, coworker affairs and marriages, and balancing family and work.

SEXUAL HARASSMENT

The biggest—or at least the most publicized—issue in offices today is sexual harassment. Employers and employees alike need to know what it is and how to deal with it.

What Is It?

The courts have ruled that there are two main elements to sexual harassment: sexual favors and a hostile work environment.

Sexual Favors

If a person in a position of authority makes sexual favors a condition of a subordinate's employment, then the subordinate is being sexually harassed. In other words, you would be a victim of sexual harassment if your boss (or another manager in the company) suggested that you have sex with him or her in exchange for keeping your job, getting a promotion, or receiving certain job-related benefits.

Hostile Work Environment

The courts have also ruled that a hostile work environment can be a form of sexual harassment. An all-male construction crew that has plastered a locker room with photos of nude women might be viewed as having created a hostile work environment.

What Can I Do?

The federal law on sexual harassment permits those who have been sexually harassed to sue their employers, but it is often possible to put an end to harassment by using other strategies. Non-legal avenues involve less wear-and-tear on the victim, especially if he or she hopes to continue working in the same place.

Handling Harassment When It Strikes

To deal with a sexual harasser, it helps to know how he or she thinks. Sexual harassers generally fall into one of two categories, and how one responds to their overtures depends on the kind of offender:

- **The Fantasist.** He or she may be seriously interested in having a relationship with—not in controlling—you. This person would like to court you, regardless of whether it is appropriate given both of your positions. This interest is genuine, and the offender is not a real sexual harasser but a pest.
- **The Realist.** This person is a real harasser. He or she is interested in obtaining sexual favors from you in exchange for advancing your career. This person usually believes that he or she is entitled to do this. This offender is harmful to you and to your job.

Question & Answer

Q: My boss keeps asking me for a date. I keep saying no. Is this sexual harassment?

A: Possibly not. It's important to know the difference between someone who is romantically interested in you and someone who is harassing you. Your boss may not be showing good judgment in asking you out, but he may not intend to harass you.

If you still receive promotions and are treated fairly at work, then your boss is not harassing you. Still, no one should be made to feel uncomfortable at work, so you may want to have a really honest talk with him in which you make it clear that while you find him a very decent person and a good boss, you are not interested in dating a fellow worker, let alone your boss.

If he continues to make unwelcome invitations, maybe you are being harassed. Talk to a lawyer, a human resources professional, or your boss's boss.

Dealing with the Fantasist

Soft approaches often work when dealing with a fantasist. This person will ask you out and even court you if given a chance. This scenario is different from that of the realist, the real sexual harasser, who invites you to his or her office, demands what he or she wants, and warns that "you can make this difficult or easy for yourself."

Here are some time-tested ways to handle the sexual fantasist:

- **Say that you are involved with someone else—only if you are.** It is a good idea to be honest about this, because it is too easy for a coworker to do some sleuthing and discover your little white lie. Then, you look bad. Of course, you could be dating someone and simply fail to mention when you break up.

- **Explain—kindly—that you do not date coworkers.** He or she will undoubtedly respond with arguments for why you should, but state your rule and stick to it. The only problem with this strategy is that if you ever do date a coworker, you'll be back where you started again.

- **Joke with him or her in front of other coworkers.** This works especially well when the overture comes from a married coworker, a not unusual situation. Say, "I'm madly in love with you. Why don't you ditch your family and we'll run away together right now?" This exercise often shakes a married fantasist out of his or her reverie. It also works with some single colleagues.

- **Use a veiled threat.** This tactic works best combined with humor. Say, "I'm madly in love with you. Let's go tell the boss that we're quitting to run away together." Most fantasist-style harassers will get the message—or get so embarrassed that they give up.

Dealing with the Realist

Unfortunately, the realist is not so easily put off; stronger measures may be called for. Before using any of them, though, try the strategies for the fantasist, just in case any of them work. If they don't, then it's time to haul out the heavy ammo, not only to slow down the harasser but also to protect yourself and build a record in the event that you find your only option is to sue.

Here are some methods to try:

- **Say "No" very clearly and sternly.** This is no time to fudge, flirt, or be funny. This person is asking you for something he or she has no right to ask you for, morally or legally. Don't leave this person with any lingering doubts about where you stand.
- **Question the offender's actions.** Ask, "Do you realize what you're doing?" or "Do you really want to do this?"
- **Take notes on your encounters.** Write down the dates, times, and locations. Write down specifically what was said. You won't want to rely on your memory if you have to recall what happened later to the harasser's boss, a human resources professional, or a lawyer. A written diary of sexual harassment carries a weight of its own.
- **Tell someone you trust what has happened.** Do this right away, so your confidante can honestly gauge your reaction. A witness can be as effective as a diary for evidence. Another reason to talk to other people is that you may discover you are not the only person being harassed. If there is a pattern of abuse in your workplace, you will have an even stronger case, to the boss or in a lawsuit.
- **Warn your harasser that you are going to make a report.** There are three very good reasons to do this. First, the warning alone may make the person straighten out. Second, this warning is fair play; anyone you report the harassment to will ask whether you have tried to work out the problem with the individual you are reporting. Third, courts are more understanding if they know you tried to deal with the situation and initiated a lawsuit only as a last resort.

- **Don't threaten to make a report if you're not going to do it.** Otherwise you're potentially setting yourself up for more harassment, because the offender won't believe you'll do anything to stop his or her advances.
- **Report the harasser's actions.** Do this after you have followed the suggestions listed earlier. In some companies, you should report harassment to a human resources professional or to another designated staff person. Where no one person or department has been appointed to deal with such issues, report sexual harassment to your boss first.

THE RIGHT PROTOCOL

Gina works in an all-female order department for a small clothing company. Her boss is touchy-feely in an inappropriate way, but none of the women dares to speak up to the boss's boss because he, too, has made passes at a few of the women.

Gina wants the women to report both bosses to the company president. Some of the women aren't sure this would be correct protocol.

Gina's idea *is* correct protocol, provided that both bosses have been warned about their activities and told that this is going to happen if they don't stop the harassing behavior.

After You Report a Sexual Harasser

Different companies respond differently to complaints of sexual harassment, but one thing is sure: All companies dread such complaints, and many try to downplay them.

Management is not always as quick and direct in its response as one might hope. Here are some tips to help you get management's attention when you report a harasser:

- **Consider consulting with a lawyer.** Just to be sure you have a legitimate case of sexual harassment, consult a specialist before you take your complaint to management.
- **Have your notes organized and your witnesses ready.** If a witness balks at supporting you under these circumstances, remind your witness that the harasser could be doing this to him or her—and probably has already done it to a lot of other people. Be prepared to name places and dates, and have direct quotations of what was said or threatened to you.

- **Complain immediately.** When harassment is regular and frequent, go to the person's boss as soon as you have determined that you have a problem. Neither bosses nor juries favor victims who report sexual harassment long after it happened; these victims are less likely to receive any compensation. If someone comes on to you once a year at the office party, however, it may take few years to see the pattern and probably is not a dangerous situation.

- **Stress that you want to be a team player.** Say that you are unhappy this has happened to you and to the company. Indicate your willingness to try to work with the company to resolve the problem.

- **Make it clear that you want the harassment to stop.** Emphasize that whereas you appreciate that this is a difficult situation for the company, you personally find it difficult, too.

- **Give the company a chance to remedy the situation.** Ask them how long they believe it will take. Also, take this opportunity to request anything that will make you feel immediately more comfortable. You may request a transfer to another department, for example.

When Legal Action Is the Only Option

Only after the company has failed at its opportunity to make amends should you take legal action. At this point, everyone has been given fair warning.

If you like your job, you should file a lawsuit only as a last resort, because there is almost no way you can feel comfortable working for a company you are suing. If you plan to do that anyway, prepare for some difficult times. You can deal with them by doing two things: hunkering down and doing your job to the best of your ability, and keeping your dignity firmly intact.

Try to keep hostilities to as low a level as possible. Do not discuss the case with your coworkers, at least not at work or in a way that will embarrass management. Don't talk about management's poor treatment of you—in fact, don't talk about management at all if you can help it. Complain to management directly if necessary.

Once management notices that you are going to continue to be discreet and considerate, they may be less likely to subject you to the non-sexual harassment that people in this situation typically encounter—which usually ends up forcing them to leave.

These approaches will help management cope with your lawsuit. More important, they help you cope with working in what could be a hostile environment.

OFFICE AFFAIRS

At the other end of the scale from the person who suffers from sexual harassment is the person who willingly becomes involved with a coworker. All the sexual harassment laws in the world will not stop human nature from taking its course. Office romances happen, and when they do, they occasionally cross some uncomfortable lines.

Any office affair will be easier on both participants and bystanders if everyone understands what is expected. There are both written and unwritten rules about office affairs. Although these vary from company to company, a few guidelines will help you handle this situation with poise:

- **Avoid involvement with inappropriate people.** In other words, do not have an affair with anyone who would create a conflict of interest (e.g., your immediate supervisor).
- **Consider requesting a transfer.** If you become involved with your supervisor and the affair appears to be long term, one of you should either arrange a transfer out of the department or look for a job at another company. It's not fair to anyone, including your coworkers, for one worker to get special treatment from the boss.
- **Be discreet, particularly at first.** Lots of people have little flings. If they don't turn into grand affairs, the fewer people who know about them, the better.
- **Don't make a big deal about it.** Even if the affair does become a grand passion, resist the temptation to announce it to the whole office. People will know you are an item, it's true, but some things are better left unsaid.
- **Arrive at and leave work separately.** This one small gesture can do a lot to protect your privacy. In the most liberal office, you will be less noticed and less a subject of gossip if you do this.
- **Treat each other like strangers at work.** Well, almost like strangers. Everyone will be watching, and they don't want to see flirtatious looks, hear jokes shared only by the two of you, and notice that you've stolen a few moments behind closed doors. The more normal you act, the more accepted the relationship will be.
- **Grant each other no special privileges.** If a meeting is scheduled to begin at 9 a.m. and your beloved has overslept, that's not your problem. Start the meeting on time. Even tiny privileges you think won't be noticed by others will be, so don't risk it.

🔍 CASE HISTORY

Bob and Diane met and married at work. They both work in the same office, although in different departments.

Over the years, they have learned a couple of tricks that help them separate work and family life. One of their favorites—partly because it so amuses their fellow workers—is to drive separate cars to work. This arrangement works particularly well because they often have schedule conflicts. For example, Bob might leave early to take their daughter to a softball game while Diane works late.

Bob and Diane also realize that their separate-car routine, as they call it, has a big social benefit, as well. It makes them look more like individuals than a married couple, which they both report is an enormous plus in the eyes of their coworkers and their bosses.

When the Affair Ends

When an office affair ends, you will wonder why you ever started the whole thing in the first place. In fact, whenever you are contemplating an office romance, it may be helpful to imagine—in advance—how you will feel when and if it does not work out.

This is where not having made a big fuss comes in handy. If you haven't made a big deal about it, you won't have to announce that it's off.

Don't gossip, badmouth, or otherwise undermine your ex-lover's work. You won't have much credibility anyway. After all, if everything about that person was delightful for six months, then you can't suddenly find everything about his or her work inappropriate and bad.

If you can't stand the reminders, ask for a transfer—to another city if need be, but certainly to a new department if you will find it hard to work around a former lover. If a transfer is out of the question, consider looking for a new job.

Office affairs used to be so taboo that when they were discovered, someone—invariably, the woman—got fired. But those were the days when women had no power. Now that women are in positions of equality with men, there are no longer any hard-and-fast rules about these situations. People don't get fired unless they have broken a company rule against dating employees or subordinates. So, often it's the person who can't stand to work around the other one who leaves to find another job.

When One or Both of You Are Married

Almost everyone is made uncomfortable by an affair between two married colleagues, and it is up to the involved couple to maintain the utmost discretion. If you must conduct this kind of affair, remember to respect your coworkers' rights:

- **Be honest.** Don't ask coworkers to lie. No one—your secretary, office mate, or anyone else—should have to cover for your absence, especially to your spouse.
- **Be discreet.** Public displays of affection in the workplace will make your coworkers uncomfortable.
- **Be fair.** Don't disappear together. Your coworkers should not have to pick up the slack because you take long lunch hours or stay out all afternoon together.
- **Be informed.** Understand that one or possibly both of you could lose your jobs as a result of your actions.

PEER FRIENDSHIPS AT WORK

Not all friendships between men and women at work are romantic. Wherever men and women work as colleagues, inevitably some real nonromantic friendships develop. Where male bonding used to take place, coworkers of both sexes now form special friendships. Nevertheless, these friendships often require a certain level of "special handling," especially if you are married and don't want to become the subject of gossip.

Outside work, you can be as tight as you like with whomever you choose, but at work, it's good protocol to exercise some restraint. Here are a few hints on how to keep your special male-female friendships from looking too special at work:

- **Plan social activities on your own time.** In other words, do your social planning outside the office.
- **Avoid exclusivity.** Don't share jokes or accord special privileges from which others are excluded.
- **Vary your lunch partners.** Occasionally go with someone else, and sometimes invite others to join both of you.
- **Don't be overly discreet.** This tactic can work against you by making it look like you have something to hide. Announce that you're having drinks together, and ask your coworkers to join you.

- **Be up-front.** If one or both of you are married, make a point of letting others know that you have met one another's spouses socially.
- **State your case and be done with it.** Some people want to believe the worst, and they'll choose to believe you are having an affair when you aren't. Don't feel obliged to protest to the rumormongers until you're blue in the face.

A Tricky Turning Point

In the most platonic friendship, there sometimes comes a moment—a night when you both work late or when you travel together—when one (and sometimes both) of you is suddenly tempted to take the friendship to the next level. Because the wisest course of action in this situation usually is to keep the friendship the way it is, someone needs to come up with an extra dose of tact if you are to remain best buddies.

For starters, if you foresee the new twist to the relationship coming, try to prevent it. Do this by dropping a few hints. Sprinkle your conversation with comments about how wonderful you think your partner or spouse is and how madly in love you are. Often a few well-timed such remarks are enough to forestall an overture that will later prove embarrassing to both of you. Remind your colleague how much you like and admire his or her partner. This tactic, too, may help your friend reevaluate his or her feelings for you. Finally, put your relationship in perspective. Say how lucky you both are to be such close friends and how sad you would be if anything happened to destroy this trust.

COWORKER MARRIAGES

These days, many people meet at work and then get married. Companies that once had policies forbidding the employment of married coworkers now accept married couples, and sometimes even try to find jobs for both partners when they started out only trying to hire one.

Nevertheless, these situations are still tricky and require some special maneuvering if other coworkers are not to resent the special ties between married coworkers. Here are some hints on handling this situation:

- **Act as if you're not married.** That's right; treat each another as if you had absolutely no relationship outside work. Don't refer to your spouse as "my wife" or "my husband." Instead, use your spouse's first name: "Bill said ..." or

"Joan suggested …" It almost goes without saying that you won't flirt, share private jokes, or otherwise carry on.

- **Avoid conferences regarding your family life.** No one expects that you'll never meet to figure out who is going to take your daughter to her soccer game, but do it quickly and discreetly.

- **Keep use of company e-mail for family communications to a minimum.** Remember that e-mail is not private. It is probably best to use the telephone for this anyway.

- **Spend less rather than more time together at work.** Don't lunch together, for example, or take breaks to chat with one another. Cultivate other social relationships.

- **Be sensitive to awkwardness about your marriage.** Coworkers may find it difficult to talk to you about a problem with your spouse. Let them know that they can—or as may be the case, cannot—do this. Best of all, of course, is to avoid all conflicts by not working in the same department or in a subordinate-superior relationship.

- **Don't intervene in an unfitting way in your spouse's work life.** For example, if someone wants you to ask your partner something that isn't part of your normal work responsibilities, refuse to do so. Send that person off to ask your spouse directly.

?? Question & Answer

Q: My husband and I work in different departments of the same company, but we occasionally work together on client presentations. Do we have to tell people that we're married?

A: There is no need to make an announcement about your relationship to your clients. On the other hand, you should not hide this fact, either. As you become friendly with clients, the subject may come up, and then it's okay to mention your ties.

PARENTING AND WORK

Not too many years ago, prejudice against working women led many of them to minimize their roles as mothers, something they felt was necessary if they were to get ahead at work—or even successfully hold a job.

A woman who needed to stay home with a sick child, for example, took a sick day for herself—and said nothing about her real reason for missing a day of work.

A recent study, fortunately, shows a drop in the number of parents who feel they have to lie about these situations.

Despite hopeful signs of change, most working parents still feel slightly guarded about their family life. They try to give the impression that they can successfully balance work and home. Here are some ways to look adept at juggling both:

- **Avoid talking too much about your children at work.** What's "too much" varies from workplace to workplace, so when you're new on the job, it's a good idea to say little until you learn what is an acceptable level of child talk.

- **Try not to discuss your children with your boss.** If he or she asks, keep comments brief and not incriminating. Otherwise, don't bring up the subject.

- **Make your children a presence at work if everyone else does it.** If others display pictures of their children or hang their drawings, feel free to do the same.

- **Be discreet when you take time out of your work day to attend to your children.** Make calls with them brief. Don't take calls from them when you're in a meeting or talking to the boss or a customer.

- **Be discreet when you take time off to attend their functions.** Inevitably, you will have to leave early occasionally to attend a soccer game or take your child to an appointment. Although you don't want to lie about your absence, don't make a point of announcing it, either.

Guidelines: Children at Work

There are times when you have no choice but to bring your child to work with you. This situation works best if your child is old enough to entertain himself or herself. Even then, it rarely works for a full day. Asking a child to play quietly for eight hours is a big request that few can fill.

If you absolutely must take Johnny with you to the office for a few hours, try to make the day go smoothly for everyone:

- **Have a master plan.** Plan how to keep Johnny happy—and out of your coworkers' hair. Bring books, drawing supplies, snacks, and some music.
- **Talk to Johnny about what you expect.** Explain that you have to work. Ask Johnny to play quietly, stay near your office, and not bother other people.
- **Keep the visit low-key.** Introduce Johnny to your coworkers, briefly explain why he is there, then say little else.
- **Don't let him interrupt.** Johnny must realize that when you are on the phone or talking with colleagues, you cannot be disturbed.
- **Move meetings out of your office.** Let someone else look in on Johnny while you have to be elsewhere. Remember, though, that no one is obliged to do this; your coworkers are not paid to be your baby-sitter. If you have to go to a meeting, instruct Johnny to play quietly for a while and tell him that Ms. Jones, your assistant, will be right outside the office if he needs anything.
- **Don't let Johnny roam around alone.** This is not appropriate for the workplace.
- **Offer a reward.** This is a boring day for Johnny, and he deserves a nice reward when it's over.

And Remember ...

- Manage your office friendships and affairs carefully. Mismanaged, they can sink a career or end a job.
- Follow strict protocol if you have to report sexual harassment. It is a serious charge and should be handled appropriately.
- Be utterly discreet when you're having a relationship with or married to a coworker.
- Make every effort to be inclusive rather than exclusive in your social interactions at work.

CHAPTER | 10

ENTERTAINING ON THE JOB

Some workers are expected to entertain business clients as one of their responsibilities, but few receive any on-the-job training about how to do it. Most learn these part-social, part-business skills by trial and error, a process that can make the most secure person feel awkward.

You need not feel this way, however, if you understand what is expected when you entertain clients. Whether it's a lunch meeting or a holiday party at the office, you should feel comfortable entertaining business associates so your guests will feel comfortable.

THE POWER LUNCH

Most business entertaining is conducted over lunch. Sometimes you'll take a customer to lunch as a thank you for his or her business, but more often, there is some wheeling and dealing to be done. In either case, it is a good idea to mention your motive when you issue the invitation.

Unlike a purely social occasion, most people who are invited to a business lunch want to know what to expect, especially if they need to do some preparation of their own.

Once you set a date with your client, call a restaurant to make a reservation, then call the client back to advise where and when to meet you. If you are sure that you won't have any difficulty getting a reservation at your restaurant of choice, then set the time and place during one phone call.

Making a Restaurant Yours

If you do a lot of business entertaining, there is nothing more helpful than patronizing one restaurant so its staff gets to know you. Then, you can be sure that you and your guests will get the royal treatment every time you dine there.

There is an art, albeit a simple one, to making yourself known at a restaurant:

- **Give your name and your company's name when you call.** Do this if you expect them to recognize you, and they will take note.
- **When you call, refer to previous visits.** Say, "This is Joe Smith. I had such a great lunch with you last week that I want to bring back another important client."
- **Claim your special table.** Say, "I want to make a reservation for lunch on Tuesday, and I'm wondering whether I can get the same booth—the one by the window—that I had last week."
- **Don't overdo it.** If the restaurant is good, they'll remember you after two or three visits, and you won't have to do anything to make your presence felt. If they don't, think about giving your business to someone who will notice your patronage.
- **Use plastic.** When you use a credit card, the staff will see, recognize, and remember your name.
- **Tip well.** Not extravagantly, but enough to be remembered. You didn't think all the special attention was going to be free, did you?

When You're The Host

Whenever you invite someone to join you in a business lunch, you are the host. It is up to you to take charge and make sure that the meal goes smoothly. Choosing a good restaurant is only the first step.

Try to arrive before your guest. If your guest should arrive early, instruct the restaurant to seat your guest and offer a drink. If you absolutely cannot make the appointed time and expect to be more than 10 minutes late, call the restaurant and ask the maître d' to advise your guest of the unforeseen delay.

Ordering Drinks

Once you are seated, the first issue is whether you drink. The rule here is simple: You may offer drinks if that practice is acceptable at your company; you probably should not offer them if it isn't. Some companies don't mind if their employees drink at lunch; others do.

Your guest takes a cue from you. If you don't offer a drink, he or she won't order one. If you order one, your guest will feel free to do the same.

When Your Guest Doesn't Drink

There are a lot fewer two-martini lunches than there used to be, partly because they are no longer totally tax deductible and partly because Americans are drinking less in general. Some people don't drink alcohol on principle, because they have a medical condition that prohibits it, or because they have a problem with it and choose to avoid it. Regardless of your guest's reason for refusing a drink, it is best not to ask.

When You Don't Drink

Sometimes the situation will be reversed: You don't drink, but you want your guest to feel free to do so. In this instance, ask your guest to order a drink without first indicating your preference. Then, order a soft drink or bottled water to accompany him or her. There is no need to explain why you aren't drinking, and the polite guest won't ask you, either.

Ordering Lunch

Your guest will look to you for guidance. He or she won't want to order more food than you do or plan for a more leisurely lunch than you have in mind. To help your guest decide, point out what's good on the menu or suggest a dish that you have enjoyed in the past. Also mention what you plan to order (e.g., a first course and an entree), then say, "Be sure to save room for dessert because it is so good here."

Some business hosts try to steer their guests toward the cheaper items on the menu, but this practice is a little crass. If you are at a nice restaurant, then you and

---

Guidelines: Alcohol

Often you must guess whether it is acceptable to your employer for you to drink at a business lunch. Here are a few clues to guide you:

- **Follow the big boss's lead.** If the president of your company does not touch alcohol, it is fairly safe to assume—unless you hear otherwise—that he or she will not be happy about paying for drinks on the company expense account.
- **Consider safety.** In some fields, people don't drink at lunch because doing so would be dangerous to their safety or to the safety of others. A construction project manager, for example, should not drink if he or she is planning to walk around on steel beams later.
- **One is sufficient.** There is no need to offer seconds on drinks at a business lunch. You may if you want to, but no one should expect it, and few people will accept in any event.
- **Buying by the bottle is okay sometimes.** Ordering a bottle of wine is okay when you're celebrating a newly signed deal, for example. Or, it may be standard practice in your business.
- **Don't make a fuss.** If you can't or don't want to drink, simply don't. Order a soft drink, bottled water, or a wine spritzer—a good harmless beverage to sip when you must keep your wits about you.
- **Keep your principles to yourself.** If you're philosophically disinclined to drink, there is no need to share this information with a customer who chooses to have a drink with his or her meal.

---

your guests ought to be free to eat anything you like. A well-mannered guest, though, will still look to you for some clue in this department, and this you will offer by mentioning what you plan to order or what you consider especially good.

If for some reason you don't care to order a full meal but don't mind if your guest does, then mention what's good without saying exactly what you are planning to order and make sure your guest orders before you do. If your guest blanches because you ordered so little, explain your order with a polite excuse: "I've been eating heavy lunches all week, so please excuse me if I eat light today."

When the food arrives, remember that as the host, you are expected to take the first bite.

If the restaurant is good, both meals will arrive at the same time. If this does not happen, you should not start eating until the other person's food arrives.

If your guest's meal arrives before yours, encourage him or her to begin eating. If your guest is really polite, he or she will wait for your meal to arrive. The only time this shouldn't be done is when it is absolutely clear that the wait will be so long that his or her food will be cold. An alternative is to send the plate back and ask the waiter to serve them both at the same time.

You are in charge of making sure that everything is okay. If your guest's steak arrives well done when he or she ordered it rare, you should ask whether he or she wants to send it back or even mention this to the waiter yourself. If anything else is not properly done, or the meal takes too long to come, you be the one to mention this to the waiter, not your guest.

Guidelines: Mealtime Etiquette

Feel like your table manners aren't quite up to snuff? The best thing you can do is buy an etiquette book and study the chapter about the etiquette at the meal table. Until you do, here are five simple dining hints that will make you look polished in any situation:

- **Use your napkin.** Put it in your lap when you sit down.
- **The utensils on the outermost edges are used first.** Work your way in from there.
- **Rest used utensils on your plate.** Never let it hang off the edge.
- **Wipe your mouth often.** Do this before taking a drink and fairly frequently while you eat, so there are no embarrassing bits of food on your face when you talk business.
- **Order only what you know how to eat.** Practice eating artichokes, lobsters, and other difficult or unusual foods at home.

Shop Talk

At a business lunch, it is expected that some business will be discussed. For this reason, you should mention to your client if your invitation is for a purely social lunch. When you discuss business is entirely at your discretion, but it is smart to keep your client's personality in mind.

Some people like to talk business over drinks, then enjoy the rest of the meal without interruption. The problem is that many people continue the discussion for the rest of the meal—which may be fine if you have a hard-driving client, but not otherwise.

Many people choose not to talk any business until everyone is finished eating. However, if you have a lot to discuss or a difficult problem to solve, there may not be enough time to really get down to business.

Try not to talk about work during the entire meal. The only exception is when you both know you need this time to talk. In this case, it is especially gracious to say, "I usually don't like to talk business while we eat, but how do you feel about doing it now, because we have so much to talk about?"

Ending the Meal

The last tricky moment of a business meal is the decision to draw it to a close. Let a business lunch go on too long, and you risk having a client who thinks you aren't very interested in work. Or, maybe your guest has to get back to work, but knows it would be rude to end the lunch before you do. Make a business lunch too short, and you lose the benefit of letting time work for you to create intimacy and trust.

A good general guideline is to remember that most business lunches don't last much longer than an hour to an hour and a half—unless you are hammering out the details of a very important deal. Either way, watch your customer for signs of restlessness, and if you see them, end the meal sooner than you planned.

It is always up to you to end the meal. Ask the waiter to bring the check, sign it, and then stand up to leave.

Who Pays?

If you issued the invitation, there is no question about who pays: It's your party, and you pick up the tab. If you frequent a restaurant, the bill will come to you automatically. Even in a new restaurant, servers tend to notice who is the host and place the bill at his or her side.

A really polite guest may make noises about paying, even though this is a purely symbolic gesture and he or she knows you won't let him pay.

Most people on expense accounts pay by credit card. If you do pay in cash, be sure you have enough to cover the bill. It is very bad form to have to borrow money to pay for a lunch you invited your customer to attend.

As you leave, you and your guest may stop together at the coat-check room. If this happens, it is a nice gesture to pay for your guest. If you leave separately, though, there's no need to worry about it.

Question & Answer

Q: I don't have any credit cards because I messed up my credit rating a few years ago, and I just started a job where I have to entertain clients. What should I do? Can I tell my boss about my situation?

A: It would most definitely not make you look like a responsible person if you tell someone who just hired you that you don't handle money well. Instead, ask for a company credit card. It is usual for a company that expects you to do any entertaining or traveling to give you one.

Saying Thank You

Because a business lunch is not purely social, you are not obliged to send a thank-you note. It is a pleasant gesture, though. So, send one if you are so inclined or if the lunch was particularly helpful, interesting, or pleasant.

When You're the Guest

When someone invites you to lunch, the entire process is reversed. You are the guest, and he or she is the host. Everything that you should do for your guests will be done for you.

OTHER OPTIONS

Lunch is the traditional way to entertain for business and perhaps the best place to discuss business, but you shouldn't be limited to it. There are various ways to entertain business clients, some of them much more appreciated and fun than lunch.

- **Breakfast.** Lots of people are fresher at breakfast or like to get an outside business meeting over with early rather than breaking up the day with it. The disadvantage is you can also end up with a sleepy, uncommunicative customer on your hands.
- **Dinner in a restaurant.** Dinner is always a more social occasion, and there definitely are times when you should entertain a client over dinner. One is when he or she is in town to meet with you and may not otherwise have

plans for the evening. Another is when you have closed a big deal and would like to celebrate.

- **Dinner at your house.** This is an excellent way to impress a client, as well as a good way to get to know him or her better in a less formal setting. Such a meal is intimate, and you should make sure it has all the earmarks of a special occasion.

- **Coffee.** Grabbing a cup of coffee can be a great way to entertain a client, especially because gourmet coffee and cappuccino bars have become extremely popular.

- **Tea.** Afternoon tea is an elegant way to entertain a client. I don't mean a cup of Salada in the local diner; rather, tea as the British take it, around 5 p.m. A fresh pot of fine tea is served with scones and clotted cream, small savory sandwiches, and individual-sized sweets. Tea is becoming increasingly popular in the United States and is served in many hotels and some restaurants.

- **Sporting events.** If you know that a client is a big fan of a certain sports team, you may have an excellent route to win favor. Many companies hold season tickets to sporting events for the express purpose of entertaining clients.

- **Concerts/plays/other live entertainment.** Not so many companies have season tickets to theaters as sporting events, but out-of-town clients who have an evening to fill might find this kind of event quite enjoyable.

Talking Business

You probably won't talk much, if any, business at a symphony concert or a basketball game. It would be a little gauche of you to then invite your guest back to the house to talk shop. It is understood that some occasions—although they are, strictly speaking, business entertainment—are for pleasure only.

Only when the opportunity presents itself and is too good to miss should you permit yourself to talk business on these more social occasions. That is, there is nothing wrong with a quick moment of business-related conversation while you're both standing in front of the grill, keeping an eye on dinner. But these opportunities present themselves; you don't make them.

INVITING THE BOSS TO DINNER

In today's fast-paced business world, inviting the boss to dinner is not the ritual it was 15 or even 10 years ago. However, in certain companies, it is still expected on occasion.

The best way to figure out whether you must—or should—invite the boss to dinner is to wait and see whether he or she invites you first. Even then, depending on the kind of dinner, you may or may not be expected to return the invitation. If your boss invites the entire department to dinner once a year, for example, then you need not worry about returning the invitation. No one would fault you for doing so, though. However, if you are invited to dinner at your boss's house alone, then you should return the invitation—either at your home or in a restaurant, as your treat.

A dinner for the boss should be as nice as any dinner you would serve a friend or a customer. If dinner parties aren't your specialty, don't try to fake it. To ensure the event goes smoothly, make reservations at a nice restaurant.

This dinner is one occasion when you don't talk business—unless the boss initiates it, of course. Even so, certain topics are off limits. You should not ask for a raise or a promotion while your boss is eating dinner at your house. Nor should you take this occasion to complain about your coworkers.

Including Partners

Any time you are entertaining a customer outside of regular business hours, you need to decide whether to include his or her partner in the invitation. If your guest brings his or her partner, then you may want to bring yours, although the days when this is required are long over. Many people's partners have busy careers of their own. For this and other reasons, many business meals do not include spouses these days.

OFFICE PARTIES

Excellent opportunities for entertaining customers, office parties are typically held during the holiday season. An inexperienced employee may be fraught with worry in anticipation, but these occasions are easy enough to handle once you have learned to maneuver your way.

First, office parties are command performances—your presence is required. You can't escape or avoid them. The least you can do is go for a short time, make your excuses ("Sorry, the baby-sitter has to be home by 8 p.m."), and take your leave.

Second, if your customers attend, they are yours to entertain. You should stay with your client, keep his or her glass and plate filled, and make sure that he or she meets interesting people.

Unfortunately, office parties have a slightly unsavory reputation, even though most are perfectly sedate. When someone makes an embarrassing mistake at an office party, it is often a young or inexperienced worker. Here's how to avoid destroying your reputation in one night at the annual office party:

- **Dress conservatively.** If the party is formal, wear formal dress to impress management. Women should wear conservative party dresses; revealing and bright-colored dresses are best saved for purely social affairs.
- **Eat and drink in moderation.** This party is not an occasion to drink and eat until you get sick. Everyone will be superficially concerned for you if you do, but the incident definitely would be held against you.
- **Share the boss.** Don't monopolize his or her time; it is too obvious a power play, besides being too boring. Your boss's job is to circulate and talk to everyone.
- **Talk to your coworkers.** You are supposed to make the rounds, too. Mix and mingle with coworkers, and thank the people you've worked with all year. You may find an opportunity, if you are so inclined, to make polite chitchat with a person you don't especially like—even find irritating—but want to butter up a bit.
- **Leave the entertainment to the entertainers.** Impromptu dirty dancing on the bar will *not* make points with coworkers or management.
- **"Get a room!"** Don't neck with anyone—even your own partner. Some people will spend the next year rehashing your antics.
- **Don't leave with anyone who could compromise your reputation.** Even if this person is only giving you a ride to the subway station, people will see, and people will talk.

EXPENSE ACCOUNTS

When you entertain people regularly for business, you will undoubtedly use an expense account. You may have a company credit card or use your own card and be reimbursed later.

THE RIGHT PROTOCOL

Karen bought a beautiful red strapless minidress that she hoped she would have a chance to wear somewhere special over the holidays. She was thrilled to learn that the annual office party was dressy, until a coworker suggested that the dress was perhaps not the most proper thing to wear. What should Karen do?

The right protocol is to save the red dress for a friend's New Year's bash and wear something more demure and professional looking to the office party. Karen might more appropriately wear something with sleeves, with a more conservative neckline, and in a more neutral color—say, brown or black, or even a sedate green or blue.

Don't play fast and loose with an expense account when you are entertaining a customer. For example, don't joke about being able to afford dinner at such an expensive restaurant "because it's the boss's tab." A smart customer will soon realize that it is not really "the boss" who's paying. That customer may not take too kindly to your frivolous attitude toward his or her money.

That said, it is perfectly acceptable to tell a client that the meal (or event) is being paid on an expense account. This might happen if you are much younger (and less powerful) than the person you are entertaining. If the customer tries to pay for the meal, without making a fuss, explain that the cost is not coming out of your pocket.

And Remember ...

- Whenever you entertain clients personally or whenever clients are entertained by your company, you are the host.
- Plan and pay for all events to which you invite clients.
- When you entertain a client, you are the one who starts talking business—and decides when to wrap it up.
- End a business meal or event in a timely manner.

CHAPTER | 11

TRAVELING ON BUSINESS

Traveling for work is different from personal traveling. In some ways, it's easier, because someone else probably will make the travel plans. The biggest difference, though, is that you are representing your company and have to act accordingly.

EXPENSE ACCOUNTS

When you travel on company business, the company pays. This is worked out in different ways at different companies. Generally, all of your travel-related expenses will be paid for—lodging, meals, and what are usually called incidental expenses.

The two most common methods of handling business travel expenses are to charge them to your personal credit card and be reimbursed by the company, or to have them billed directly to a company account. Some companies prefer to use a per diem instead of an open-ended expense account. This is a set dollar amount that you are allowed to spend each day. If the per diem, for example, is $100 a day, and the room costs $75, you are left with $25 to cover meals and incidental expenses.

Incidentals

Incidental expenses are the trickiest expenses to deal with when you travel for work. In theory, everything you buy specifically for the trip should be expensed. In reality, companies find some expenses more acceptable than others.

The following list will give you some sense of what can be charged to your expense account and what cannot.

Probably Chargeable	**Probably Not Chargeable**
Weekday newspaper	Sunday newspaper
Business magazine	Fashion magazine[1]
Toothbrush, hairbrush, and comb	Travel case to hold them
Late-night snack of chips and salsa	Caviar
Bottle of wine	Bottle of champagne
Tote bag[2]	Fancy leather briefcase
Warm socks or tights[3]	Flannel nightgown

[1] Unless you work in the fashion industry.
[2] To be used to carry back work-related goods obtained during the trip.
[3] Needed because the weather takes a nose dive.

Life on an Expense Account

How you travel for work may or may not match your personal travel style—and the difference can go either way. People who like to fly first class and stay in luxury lodgings when traveling on their own might be appalled to hear that the boss expects them to fly tourist class and stay in pretty basic hotels when traveling on business.

In pleasant contrast, some companies allow their employees a certain amount of luxury when they travel. This perk usually comes with a job for which a great deal of travel is required or when you meet with clients that the company is eager to impress.

Sometimes, travel perks are based on rank, which means that the executives travel first class, while everyone else travels business class.

Use It—Don't Abuse It

Expense accounts are meant to be used when you travel. If you're new to traveling on business, don't hesitate to use it, but only when it's appropriate. Keep accurate records of your expenses, and maintain your expenses within reasonable limits.

If you abuse your expense account by eating every meal in an expensive restaurant and by charging a lot of "incidentals," your boss may be less than eager to let you represent the company.

Getting caught in a flagrant lie on your expense account can be grounds for firing.

PLANNING AND TRAVEL

One of the nicest things about work-related travel is that someone else—a travel agent—will probably plan your trip for you. Very few companies expect their employees to make their own travel arrangements, so your first question upon learning that you will be taking a trip on the company's behalf will be to ask who will book the trip.

Using a Travel Agent

Even if the company doesn't have its own travel agent, you would be well-advised to find one to make your arrangements. Travel agents are paid commissions by hotels and airlines and usually do not pass along expenses to their clients, so you have nothing to lose—except some headaches—by using one.

The second question you should ask is how you are expected to travel, that is, business class or tourist class. So as not to appear too naive (or worse, greedy), you should not ask your boss this question directly; rather, try to absorb the information from someone else.

A travel agent who regularly handles travel arrangements for the company will know the company's policy regarding employee travel. Your boss's secretary or administrative assistant is another good source of information, as will be any employee who regularly travels on business.

Travel agents are sources of other kinds of information, too, so don't hesitate to ask about the weather, restaurants, and dress in your destination city.

To help your travel agent plan the best possible trip for you, follow these simple guidelines:

- **Allow enough time to plan the trip.** Except in emergencies, call to book your travel two to three weeks—even a month—before your departure date. The agent can thus find the best air fares.
- **Have the exact dates of travel at hand when you call.** If you are flexible by a day or two in either your departure or return date, say so. There may be a significant difference in fares on two different dates.
- **State what time of day you prefer to travel.** If you will find it impossible to make a 7 a.m. flight, for example, say so during your first conversation.
- **Be prepared to offer other preferences, too.** The agent probably will ask whether you prefer an aisle or a window seat. You also can make other requests, for example, a seat up front or in the back of the plane, or a special meal.

THE RIGHT PROTOCOL

Julie became friendly with the travel agent who booked all her business travel, so much so that she made a few flippant comments about her expense account. Specifically, she said she could charge her entire work wardrobe to her expense account and the company probably wouldn't notice. To her surprise, then shock, her comments reached her boss's ears. He let her know in an off-handed way that he found them embarrassing. Julie wasn't sure what she'd done wrong. Did she breach protocol?

Julie did breach protocol because she confided in the wrong person by assuming an intimacy—and therefore a loyalty—that didn't exist.

The travel agent's client was the company, personified in Julie's boss. Although lots of travel agents would have let the comments pass (and maybe this one meant no harm in passing them on), like any good salespeople, travel agents forge liaisons with their customers.

In this case, Julie's boss's secretary and the travel agent had become good friends, and this worked against Julie. Julie was wrong not to realize where the travel agent's loyalties could lie, and she was wrong in not being more discreet.

Planes and Trains

When you travel on business, you are representing your company, so it helps to have some sense of how to conduct yourself as a business traveler. Here are some tips:

- **Be polite.** That means everyone who helps you, from the travel agent who plans your trip to the flight attendant who serves you dinner.
- **Order special meals in advance.** Do this when you book your flight. Most airlines offer a variety of special meals, including low-fat, or low-calorie, kosher, diabetic, pork-free, and vegetarian.
- **Arrive on time.** Your boss won't be impressed to hear that you missed your plane.
- **Quietly enjoy business class.** Don't abuse the privilege. In other words, order a nice wine, but skip the champagne if you think your boss might not go for it. Don't eat or drink so much that you risk getting sick on the plane.
- **Show some discretion.** Do not discuss company business in a public place, such as an airport waiting room, restaurant, or on the plane itself. During the week, planes and trains are filled with business travelers—and your competition could be sitting across the aisle from you.
- **If you need to work or sleep, say so.** The days are gone when travelers whiled away the hours sharing life stories, but you just may encounter a chatty seatmate. It is perfectly acceptable to explain that you cannot talk. You can either say this directly or simply give curt, fairly unresponsive replies to any questions you are asked in hopes that the person will get the message. Alternately, try reading.

Hotel Safety Smarts

Another issue for those whose work forces them to travel—especially women—is that of traveling safely. The entire travel industry has awakened to the fact that more women are traveling for business, often unaccompanied, and it has taken steps to improve safety.

There are a few precautions that anyone can take to stay safe when traveling:

- **Stay in a hotel instead of a motel.** Unlike a motel, a hotel features a common lobby, often has an attached parking garage, and may provide valet parking. All these are safer than parking your car in an isolated parking lot behind the building and entering your room from the outside.
- **Say nothing about staying alone.** Don't mention it to strangers or to clients unless you know them well.
- **Don't let clerks announce your room number to the entire hotel lobby.** If this happens, quietly ask for another room.

- **Let a bellhop show you to your room.** The bellhop should walk around the room to make sure it is unoccupied. Make sure all closets and the bathroom are empty before the bellhop leaves.
- **Check the security features.** Make sure the door's double lock, chain, and/or deadbolt works and that the windows lock. Especially if you're a woman traveling solo, make sure that no one can reach your window from the outside. If anything is wrong with the room's security, ask for another room.
- **Secure the door when you're inside.** Never open your door to an uninvited visitor. Ask who it is, and if the visitor claims to be hotel staff, call the front desk to verify.
- **Make friends with the staff, so they'll look out for you.** Don't overdo it, though, for obvious reasons—you won't want any unwelcome visits from them, either.
- **Don't befriend strangers, especially in a city.** Doing so makes you an easy mark.
- **Be aware of who is around you.** When going to your room, look over your shoulder. If anyone suspicious is behind you, keep walking—right back to the lobby.
- **Never enter your room if the door is open or unlocked.** For that matter, if there's anything suspicious about the room, get out. Go back to the lobby, and ask someone to accompany you.

GETTING TO WORK

The purpose of your trip is to conduct business, so you should be prepared for it. Several things require advance planning; others you can take care of when you arrive:

- **Plan for equipment needs.** If you require certain equipment or materials to make a sales presentation, arrange in advance to either ship it to your destination or rent it when you get there.
- **Arrange a meeting room.** Look into this before you arrive. Ask whether the hotel has a conference room you can book, or investigate other resources. It is not advisable, especially for women, to conduct business in a hotel room. The only exception is if you are staying in a hotel that offers business suites.

🔍 CASE HISTORY

When Tasha arrived at her hotel at midnight, after a delayed airline flight, there was no bellhop available to show her to her room. She decided to find it by herself—after all, she frequently stayed at this hotel and knew it well. To her horror, when she opened the door to the room she had been assigned, it was occupied—by a woman as terrified as she was.

Tasha returned to the front desk, got a key to another room, and amazingly enough, found an occupant in that room, too.

Wondering what she could do to remedy this frightening situation, Tasha headed back to the desk yet again. She didn't really want to find another hotel in the middle of the night, but she was annoyed and frightened. She decided to ask for another room and insist that a staff person, if not a hotel manager, accompany her to it. She still did this quietly, though, so as not to draw attention to herself in a hotel lobby late at night.

The next day, Tasha filed a formal complaint with the hotel management. If they weren't responsive, she planned to find another hotel for her next visit.

These suites typically are designed with the bedroom in the back and a combination living room and conference room in the front.

- **Consult your client.** If you know your client fairly well, you might ask to borrow equipment or use one of the company's offices for a presentation; however, don't assume that this will be possible. Your client may even suggest meeting in his or her office, so if there's no good reason not to, then accept the gracious offer.

- **Overpack.** Go against everything you were taught and take more samples, reports, or demos than you think you will need. Nothing is more painful than listening to a business traveler explain why he or she didn't bring the new sample case—when that was the entire point of the sales call, from the customer's point of view.

- **Arrive on time for the meeting.** Fly in the night before if you have to. If it's winter and the weather is likely to be bad, leave extra travel time. The fact that you have flown 5,000 miles or that your plane arrived at 3 a.m. instead of 7 p.m. is no excuse for tardiness. The bigger and more important the meeting, the more important it is that nothing interfere.

- **Don't act lonely.** It doesn't inspire confidence in your professional skills. A client is not obliged to entertain you or even to have dinner with you for other than business purposes, so find something else to do with your down time. If the subject comes up, let the client know you've got someplace to be. You'll look pleasantly self-sufficient.

❓ Question & Answer

Q: I'm a woman and travel as part of my job. Recently, a fairly new male client suggested to me several times that we have drinks after dinner in my room. I said no, but I know he'll repeat the invitation the next time I see him. What can I do?

A: Follow your instincts: Keep saying no. Most late-night offers of drinks or visiting your room aren't about work.

The real trick is to say no both graciously and firmly. Try saying thanks but no thanks, and then change the subject before your client has a chance to pursue it. If his passes become more direct, you can always explain that you don't date clients.

CONVENTIONS

Conventions are a popular form of business travel. Companies often try out inexperienced or new employees with this form of travel before sending them out on their own.

All too often, conventions are viewed as one big office party, a time to cut loose—although nothing could be further from the truth. Companies send employees to conventions to represent them, and they often expect a great deal of work from them, too.

Because all levels of employees attend conventions, they can provide you with an opportunity to show off your abilities in front of a boss or some other mentor. Make sure you get noticed for your quick thinking in an emergency or your problem-solving prowess, rather than your ability to chug down drinks at the party your company gives to entertain its big clients. If you want to make a name for yourself as a valued employee at conventions, follow a few simple rules:

- **Do your job.** Show up to man the convention booth when you're supposed to (and even when you're not, if you really want to impress). Volunteer to lend a hand at a sales meeting or a seminar conducted by a fellow employee.

> ### 🔍 CASE HISTORY
>
> Janet had traveled from Milwaukee to Chicago to make a presentation to a prospective new client. She had arranged for the hotel to have a slide projector available, but when she arrived at her hotel, she was told that none was available—even though she had been assured that one would be.
>
> Janet was in a quandary about what to do, because she wanted everything to go smoothly so she could impress her potential customer. Her first thought was to throw herself at the client's mercy, but because she had a couple of hours, she first tried to rent a projector.
>
> When Janet couldn't round up the equipment, she called the client, who said he was happy to let her use his. He added that he was impressed with her perseverance and the fact that she had tried an alternate route first.

- **Speak well of your company.** Remember that you are its representative wherever you go. Don't badmouth the boss or the company to strangers or, worse, to potential or actual clients.
- **Follow the crowd.** When everyone goes out to dinner, a concert, or a play together, go along—even if you're exhausted from being with people all day and would like nothing better than to go back to your hotel room and watch a movie on cable.
- **Don't flirt.** With anyone—employees or customers. A certain kind of freedom does flower at conventions, and women especially may find themselves in unexpectedly compromising situations. This may, for example, be the moment when the head of sales decides to make a play for a colleague, even though he's always been circumspect before. One of the best ways to avoid awkward situations is to prevent them. Act professional to everyone at all times. Realize that even the slightest flirtation—which under other circumstances would never be misinterpreted—could be seen in another light.

ENTERTAINING

If you have a genuine reason to entertain a client while you're out of town, then by all means do so. Take charge of the arrangements just as if you were on your home turf. You extend the invitation, suggest the locale, and make reservations or buy tickets. During the dinner or the event, you act as host.

One good reason to entertain a client is when you have just concluded a big deal. In this case, the dinner will be celebratory. You should choose a very nice restaurant and order champagne or a fine wine.

And Remember ...

- When you travel on business, you represent your employer at all times.
- It is up to the company to set standards for business travel.
- To minimize stress and maximize your chances of getting the travel arrangements you prefer, prepare for your trip well in advance of your departure date whenever possible.
- Conduct yourself professionally during all business travel.

CHAPTER | 12

WRITING STILL REQUIRED

Even with new modes of communication—and the informality they have brought to written communications—it still is necessary to have business writing skills.

Writing skills help you organize your thoughts as well as your reports and memos. You will be a more versatile employee if you understand how to think and write your way through business documents.

HONING YOUR SKILLS

Formal business communications are conducted in a certain style. Underlying all good business writing are the rules of grammar and spelling as well as an ability to organize one's thoughts and then put them on paper in a logical order that flows well.

If you feel you lack the skills to prepare well-written documents, one of the best things you can do for yourself is to obtain them. You can learn these skills from a book, or you could take a course in business writing. The business section of any good bookstore will contain a selection of books about writing business letters, memos, and reports.

If you already write well, you will find it helpful to keep some writing tools handy at your desk. These include a good high school or college grammar book, a dictionary, and possibly a thesaurus.

Another excellent way to learn is by example. Take time to study the well-written reports and letters that come across your desk and learn to recognize what makes them so effective.

THE BUSINESS LETTER

The most common business document is the business letter. It is typed (or printed from the computer) on company letterhead. A business letter contains several parts: heading, date, inside address, greeting, body, closing, and signature. A sample letter is shown on page 127.

Heading

The heading of a business letter will probably be pre-printed on company stationery. If it isn't, type it in. Company letterheads contain far more information than they used to. Telephone number, fax number, e-mail address, and Web site (URL) are now commonly seen on letterheads.

Date

It's always important to date business correspondence. This may be necessary to help you know when to follow up; it also creates a paper trail that may be used in litigation or other settlement of disputes.

Dating a letter establishes when an action was first taken regarding a complaint or some other aspect of business and reveals whether the action was taken in a timely fashion.

Inside Address

The inside address contains the name, street address, city, state, and ZIP code of the person to whom you are writing. There is no need to include a telephone or fax number, or an e-mail address—even if you are faxing or e-mailing the letter.

Heading	Lenore Dress Company
	2 West Oak Street
	Chicago, Illinois 60603
	Telephone: 313-857-9573
Date	July 2, 2004
Inside Address	Mr. Seymour William
	32 W. Fulton Circle
	Chicago, Illinois 60634
Greeting	Dear Mr. William:
Body	We are sorry to learn that your recent order was unacceptable to you. We have asked your regular sales representative Mary Michael to call on you personally next week to discuss your problem.
	I am confident that Ms. Michael will be able to resolve your difficulty; however, should this not be the case, please feel free to contact me personally.
Closing	Sincerely,
Signature	Jeff Cyrus

Greeting

The greeting in a social letter is followed by a comma ("Dear Seymour,"). In a business letter, a colon is used, even if you are on a first-name basis.

Use titles and last names when writing to someone you do not know personally—at least the first time you write to that person. If "Dear Mr. William:" sounds too formal, you can write "Dear Seymour William:" instead.

Only if you are on a first-name basis with someone should you refer to your addressee by first name only in correspondence.

Body

The body of the letter is what really counts. It should contain all the information you want to convey—in plain English.

Two basic formats are commonly used. One is to indent every paragraph, as is done in the sample letter. Usually with this style, no extra space is added between the paragraphs. The other is to make all paragraphs flush left (no paragraph indent) and then put one line space between paragraphs.

Business letters are always single-spaced and typed.

Because people seem to have little time to read today, it's a good idea to try to keep your business correspondence brief. Most letters run only one page, certainly not more than a page and a half.

Closing

"Sincerely" has become the standard closing these days, but "Regards" and "Warmest Regards" are also acceptable, particularly when you have a special relationship with someone.

Husbands and wives (or lovers) who write business documents to each other should take care to avoid intimacies; signing all their business correspondence "Sincerely," is probably a good practice. Even if you are unusually friendly or on otherwise intimate terms with the person to whom you're writing, think twice about being too informal—or too intimate—so as not to call attention to yourselves.

CASE HISTORY

Gerry, a young editor who was having an affair with his boss, learned his lesson the hard way. Never imagining that anyone would read the correspondence he wrote to his boss, he signed his memos and notes to her "Hugs and Kisses."

However, a book they worked on together became the subject of litigation. As a result, their letters were read in open court. Not only did the letters embarrass both of the involved parties, but they also helped the defendants to win their case—by revealing that the boss had covered up Gerry's mistakes because of her personal involvement with him.

Signature

Below the closing, sign your name and then type it. You should always type your full name (i.e., your first and last names) rather than only your first name. You may, however, sign just your first name if you are a on a first-name basis with the person to whom you're writing. If you are not, or if this is your first exchange of letters, then use your formal signature.

Additional Information

Business letters also sometimes contain other specialized information. The most popular additions are the following:

cc: Jane Dickson
Trevor Jones

and

Encl.: 4 pp.

A term that has become technically irrelevant, "cc" means "carbon copies" and indicates that you are sending copies of the letter to the below-named persons. Even if you are sending e-mail copies, it's a good practice to note who is being sent copies.

"Encl." is an abbreviation for "Enclosure" and indicates that something has been attached or included in the envelope. "Att." (for "Attached") is now as commonly used as "Enclosure," especially when documents are faxed, and the number of pages may or may not be noted.

TITLE WARS

These days, with informality the prevalent social form of office behavior, there tends to be less and less use of titles such as "Mr.," "Mrs.," and even "Ms." Some people take pride in eliminating titles entirely from business correspondence, preferring to start letters with "Dear John Smythe:" for example. Still, titles are appropriate under certain circumstances and can even earn you some mileage if you're trying to impress. Here are some examples of occasions when it is a good idea to use titles:

- **When it's a new contact.** You have never met the person you're writing to, and this is the first correspondence you have had with him or her.

- **When you write to a much older person.** This person might be old enough to expect the use of a title.
- **When you, a subordinate, are writing to a superior.** This rule applies even when you write to a superior at another company.
- **When you write on behalf of your superior.** Use titles as a form of deference and respect.

Which Should You Use?

"Mr." is the usual title for any male over the age of 12. "Mrs." is used with married women, even though the purpose of "Ms."—which was invented in the 1970s—was to eliminate any distinction between married and unmarried women. (There is, after all, none for men.)

Many people use "Mrs." for married women and "Ms." for unmarried women. A surprising number of people still object to the use of "Ms." because of its shades of feminism, even though its use is now accepted by some very conservative institutions—notably, law firms and *The New York Times*.

The title "Dr." is used in business correspondence for medical doctors and doctors of other persuasions—anyone who has a Ph. D., for example. "Esquire" (often shortened to "Esq.") is used for lawyers.

 Question & Answer

Q: My boss hates the title "Ms.," but I think it's old-fashioned and even a little sexist to use anything else. What should I do?

A: When you write letters that go out with your boss's signature, follow his wishes and use "Mrs." and "Miss." In letters that go out with your signature, you may use "Ms.," with one exception: If your boss will be reading those letters, why go out of your way to aggravate him?

When you're the boss, you can do whatever you like.

MEMOS AND REPORTS

In truth, the difference between a memo and a report are very slight. Normally, though, a memo is circulated in a department or within the company. It is considered less formal than a report, which is more likely to be distributed to the top brass or to entities outside the company. Having said this, though, all memo writers should keep in mind that any memo has the potential to be upgraded to a report.

Memos and reports are more formal than the e-mail communications people send off on a whim without much forethought or rewriting. They are excellent modes of communication, sometimes better than e-mail or conversation, both of which can be too spontaneous. People take time to write them, and readers have time to absorb the information they contain before they respond to them.

One difference that may help you prepare these communications is that memos are frequently used to put forth suggestions or to persuade someone to some future action, whereas a report is often a compilation of an action or program that already has been put in place.

The same general guidelines can be used to shape both documents:

- **Limit your topic.** Few people will have the time or the inclination to hear all your views on all aspects of business operation in one report. It's wise to limit memos and reports to one clearly identified subject.

- **Keep it brief.** Memos and reports are often longer than business letters, but both are shrinking in size these days. The average report or memo—except for those treating very complex subjects—rarely runs longer than 15 to 20 pages, and many very effective ones are only 3 or 4 pages long. Here's a hint: Write only as much as you need to, and don't worry about how long it is. It is not a term paper, and you will not lose points for writing fewer words; in fact, if your document is well written, people will appreciate your conciseness. Don't waste your readers' time with irrelevant prose.

- **Outline before you write.** An outline gives you an opportunity to help clarify your thoughts and make sure you are raising interesting, pertinent points. It also gives you a structure to follow as you work, to keep you from straying from your topic.

- **Avoid extremes.** Skip words that are overly powerful or emotional. Words such as "threaten," "hate," "love," or even "should" have unwelcome connotations in a business document. You do not want to come across as passionate or overwrought.

- **Don't overdo it.** Use plain, down-to-earth language. Avoid jargon (except for that in your field, which will be understood by all readers), long words where shorter alternatives will do, and flowery phrases. Save it all for your great novel.

- **Avoid phrases that sound pompous.** Phrases such as "of course," "as you know," "obviously," and "as I was saying" sound affected in print, if not necessarily in conversation.
- **Make sure it's clean and neat.** Handwritten notes and corrections are messy. (With a computer, why would you need to write on the page anyway?) Print the memo or report, double-space it if it runs more than a couple of pages, use wide margins, and consider using subheads if it's lengthy and complicated.
- **Check your grammar and spelling.** An unintentional typographical or spelling error makes your document look unprofessional and less credible.
- **Proofread it.** Check and double check any memo or report several times before sending it out.

A final word: When something important is at stake—like when you're trying to persuade the company to start a new division that you hope to head—have an unbiased reader (a friend, family member, or coworker) check the report or memo before you send it out. Even when the stakes aren't very high, consider having another pair of eyes look at your work before you distribute it.

It behooves you to choose this person carefully, for a couple of reasons. The most important is that you want honest yet tactful feedback, not criticism from an office underminer. The second is that you have to trust that the person who reads your work won't steal your ideas.

Guidelines: Persuasive Language

The point of most memos and reports is to sell an idea or a suggestion. To this end, persuasive language will earn you a lot of points. Be sure to use lots of it in your memos and reports.
Some effective phrases include the following:

- "Here is the problem I've spotted."
- "Several solutions are possible."
- "I believe the best solution is to ..."
- "The advantages of Plan A are ..."
- "I recommend the following:"

Guidelines: Action Verbs

All memos and reports are more effective and easier to read when you use action verbs, active constructions, and specific (not vague) language. Here are some examples:

Instead of:	Say:
"It has occurred to me ..."	"I think (believe, know) ..."
"Some people say ..."	"The president said ..."
"Workers were denied an opportunity ..."	"Management denied workers ..."
"The ball was dropped ..."	"We dropped the ball ..."

And Remember ...

- Make sure your business letters, memos, and reports are clean, neat, and either typed or printed on the computer (not hand-written), with no spelling or grammatical errors.
- Think, plan, and outline before you write.
- Use your head, not your heart—business writing is clear and concise, not emotional.
- Err on the side of formality. There will always be room for informality later.

CHAPTER | 13

SPEAKING OUT

At work, as in the rest of your life, you are judged to a great extent by how you speak—the sound of your voice as well as how you express yourself. Careers have been brought to a dead halt by an unpleasant speaking voice. And they have also been unduly—or even duly—advanced by an unusually pleasant speaking voice. Most of us know someone who is considered a riveting speaker because his or her voice is so beautiful or unusual, and we usually like to be around this person.

What does it take to have a voice that people like to listen to?

WHAT YOU DON'T KNOW CAN HURT YOU

Most people who have screechy, high-pitched, or nasal voices don't even realize it. One way to find out what your voice sounds like to others is to ask a friend—but be sure to ask a friend who will give you an honest answer.

Another way is to try to judge for yourself. If you think you can do this, tape record your voice and play back the tape. How do you sound?

The best way to find out for sure may be to spend an hour or so with a speech coach, who can identify your problem, if you have one, and measure its seriousness.

Big Problems

Before you can begin to correct your speech, you have to identify what's wrong with it. There are several common speech flaws.

Through the Nose

The most common speech flaw is excessive nasality, which runs through many regional accents, ranging from the local speech in New York City to dialects in such diverse locations as Chicago and Kansas City. A nasal voice makes the most happy-go-lucky person sound like a whiner, so it's especially important to correct this habit.

Made for Speed

At opposite ends of the speech spectrum are people who speak too slowly and those who speak too quickly. Both problems affect how others hear you.

Listeners may grow impatient listening to slow speakers and eventually begin to tune them out. Or, more maddening, they interrupt and finish sentences for them. Fast speakers run their words together so that they are difficult to understand. Sometimes their listeners do not realize that they are speaking English.

Volume Control

Your teachers were right when they encouraged you to neither yell nor fade away. Both are aggravating speech patterns. The loud voice grates, and people want to get away from it. The soft voice carries little or no authority and can be annoying to a listener who has to keep leaning forward, trying to get closer to the source.

Project your voice enough that you can be heard, but don't yell; speak loudly enough that people don't constantly ask you to repeat what you have just said.

(Mumble, Mumble)

Somewhat akin to the soft speaker is the mumbler, who slurs words *and* speaks very softly. This kind of voice sounds bland, and like the soft speaker, is not authoritative. It is not a good voice for an aspiring executive, because people can't understand a word of it.

Correcting the Biggies

If you have a major speech problem, it is definitely in your best interest to do something to correct it. In fact, your career may depend on it.

Time takes care of some speech problems. Some people lose nasality when they are not around nasal speakers, and some people learn to speak up and not to mumble as they naturally gain authority. If this does not happen to you, then you may need to make an extra effort.

Spending a couple of hours a day practicing modulation and enunciation is sometimes enough to set you on the right path. You also might study some books about improving your speech. Use a tape recorder to practice what you learn. Another idea is to use English language tapes (the kind that foreign speakers use to learn English) to improve your speech. The speakers on these tapes will have good voices to emulate. Some are specifically targeted for non-native speakers who want to improve their accents—see if your local library or bookstore has a copy.

Often, speech problems are difficult to correct by yourself. If you want outside help, look into speech classes or hiring a speech coach to work with you one-on-one. The money will be well spent.

Speech that Sets You Apart

Many people today have speech tics or habits that could be easily corrected if they would simply take the time and make the effort to train themselves. Learning what is acceptable will make you sound like one of the crowd instead of an interloper.

Filler Words

The most popular tic is the repetitive use of meaningless words and phrases such as "you know," "okay," and "um" to fill in between the things you say that actually mean something.

These and a steadily changing roster of other currently popular speech tics, such as "like" and "really," are also part of youth culture, so you should make a special effort to minimize their use when you start working.

Youthspeak

If you're young and just starting your first job, one of the things you'll have to decide is how much "youthspeak" is advisable to keep in your speech. How you modify your speech (or not) will depend on the environment where you work.

Although many of the expressions young people use today are amazingly inventive, they are often seen by some adults as badges of immaturity. If you sense that your youthful speech offends coworkers yet you want to get ahead, it would be wise to limit such use to weekends and other occasions when you're with your peers.

Spanglish

The combination of English and Spanish that many young people speak (as well as minority dialects and other language combinations with English) is better reserved for conversations with your peers outside of work. This speech is unintelligible to people who do not speak the language (or languages).

Spanglish and minority dialects are marvelously inventive, but they are not easily understood by mainstream English speakers. Thus, they may give offense by making people—specifically, your boss and coworkers—feel left out.

Jargon

A specialized vocabulary that applies to only one field, jargon also can hold you back at work. Legalese is a kind of jargon, as is the special language that computer experts have created. Jargon is the refuge of the insecure, a group that often includes new or young workers who tend to overuse it.

Even if you work for a computer technology company or a law firm, your boss may find it annoying if you speak nothing else but technical jargon. He or she may wonder whether you are capable of communicating in plain English. Your customers may not only dislike jargon but actively resent it, especially if they don't understand what you're saying.

Think twice before you overuse and abuse jargon. There are better ways to reveal your intelligence.

Regional Accents

Largely because of television, regional accents are fading away in American life. We still have northern and southern accents, and host of others—but linguistics experts report that Americans are sounding more and more alike than ever before.

Television commentators, reporters, and actors speak "standard English," which is rapidly becoming the accent of choice across the country. The question for you, especially if you go to work in another part of the country, is whether you want to keep the hometown twang or lose it in favor of sounding more like your new peers.

If you live where there is a strong local accent, there may in fact be no reason to lose it. It may even work to your advantage in business. However, if, like the vast majority of Americans, you no longer live where you learned your regional accent, you may feel more comfortable losing it. An out-of-place accent can work against you in a new town, just as it can work for you in its place.

Some people lose local accents without even realizing it. Some people also are more susceptible than others to picking up others' speech patterns. A few people have to make a concerted effort to lose a regional accent. If you're one of the latter, listen carefully and study other people's speech to determine how you should change the way you speak. You may have to modify vocabulary, speed, and volume, for example.

Behavior that Sets You Apart

Some behaviors related to conversational style differ by region or by cultures. Any time that you plan to travel to another part of the world, take some time to study the characteristics of conversation. This way, you will not be offended, because you understand what is expected of you. You also will not offend by simply doing what comes naturally to you.

Body Language

All cultures have unspoken standards regarding body language. In many Asian countries, for example, it is considered rude to keep your hands in your pockets while speaking to another person. This custom doesn't bother Americans at all. Some cultures expect a lot of gesticulation from speakers. Americans expect less, rather than more, body language from speakers.

In our culture, too much body language is widely perceived as making someone a less effective speaker. People tend to watch the speaker's hands rather than listen to what is being said; listeners often are distracted by a lot of body movement.

Here are some hints to help you tone down your body language:

- **Control your hand gestures.** Keep your hands in your lap when you're seated and at your sides when you're standing. Don't flail them about.
- **Stand (or sit) tall.** Don't fidget or shift your weight from leg to leg. When sitting, avoid crossing and uncrossing your legs.

- **Go your grooming beforehand.** Don't rearrange your hair or pick at your clothing while you're speaking.
- **Face your listener.** Don't turn your back to someone while speaking. Turn around to face him or her, if at all possible.
- **Keep your feet down.** Don't sit with the sole of your shoe facing up toward someone's face. Most of the world considers this a rude gesture, and while Americans have no formal prohibition against it, it can have a slightly disrespectful quality.

Distance

Depending on the culture, people expect more or less physical distance between speakers. If you go against a cultural norm, you will make the person you're speaking to extraordinarily uncomfortable. If your custom is to stand close when speaking and the person you're speaking with is used to standing farther apart, you will perform quite a dance as the conversation continues. You will instinctively keep moving closer while the other will keep stepping away.

People from the Middle East, for example, stand very close together, by American standards, when they speak. Americans, in contrast, like more distance. Sometimes, for whatever reason, a person does not learn the cultural norm in his or her own culture and stands too close or too far away when talking to people. Observe your own behavior to determine whether you maintain the preferred distance. If you don't, strive to do so.

Body Contact

Another cultural aspect among speakers is body contact. Americans are a low-contact people, whereas in many other parts of the world, people commonly kiss when they greet and/or touch one another on the shoulder or arm for emphasis or to achieve intimacy when they speak. If you sense that your level of body contact makes other people uncomfortable, you should try to modify it.

Eye Contact

Eye contact, like body language, varies from culture to culture and even within various ethnic groups in the United States. Among African Americans, for example, it is often considered rude for a child to look directly at a parent or other adult who is chastising them. In contrast, most white Americans tend to consider it a sign of disrespect if a child does not look directly at them while they are speaking.

As a general rule, adult Americans like and expect direct eye contact between two speakers. Thus, if you come from a culture or an ethnic group where this is not the norm, it's a good idea to adopt the more mainstream form of eye contact.

THE ART OF CONVERSATION

As important as displaying good speaking habits is the ability to converse well. A lot of talking goes on in offices, and you'll want to know how to do it right.

Here are some hints on making conversation:

- **Keep it interactive.** Encourage the participation of the person to whom you are speaking. Do this by asking questions such as, "What do you think?" and "Can you give me an example?"
- **Don't rattle.** Many people talk too freely and too much. Learn to think, and even to weigh your thoughts, before you speak.
- **Stick to the bare facts.** Most people give too many facts and details, especially when speaking to a superior. Pare down what you have to say, and your opinions will be more respected.
- **Share the wealth.** Especially at work, it's important to give credit where it's due. Never use "I" when "we" is more appropriate. Refer to "the committee" and "the team," not "my committee" and "my team." Overuse of the first person (i.e., "I" and "my") makes you look selfish and not much of a team player.
- **Give way.** Interruption isn't all bad—in fact, in some circles it's a sign of lively conversation—but it can get out of hand and be annoying, especially when it's a persistent speech trait in a young or inexperienced worker speaking to a superior or an older person. Interruptions are more acceptable in some parts of the country than in others.

Guidelines: Interruptions

Here are four hints to keep you from interrupting others:

1. Don't ask irrelevant questions.
2. Don't make irrelevant remarks.
3. Don't finish someone else's sentence.
4. Don't add unimportant details.

- **Agree; don't argue.** Argumentative people aren't much loved; good-natured people are. It's that simple. Even when you disagree with someone, tell them gently. Instead of exclaiming, "You're dead wrong about that" or "I don't believe that (or you)," try "You may be right" or "That's a good idea, but how about this?"

The Art of Listening

Dorothy Sarnoff, a well-known speech coach, once wrote that 50 percent of good conversation was *listening*. Many a mediocre or uninformed speaker has been considered a brilliant conversationalist simply because he or she knew how to really listen.

This skill is definitely worth cultivating. Here's how:

- **Turn to face the speaker.** Showing him or her your back is a rude gesture.
- **Make frequent eye contact.** Eye contact shows your interest in what the speaker has to say.
- **Look lively.** Let changes in your facial expression—delight, amazement, surprise—break through.
- **Don't plan too far ahead.** Avoid thinking about what you're going to say while someone else is still speaking.

CASE HISTORY

Jay wanted to praise his boss for a brilliant speech he had just given to the entire company, but the boss was mobbed with people. Besides, Jay didn't want to be one more face in the crowd. He thought that if he said the speech was great—which it was—the boss would say thank you, and that would be the end of it. Jay, who had made it a point to listen very carefully to his boss's speech, was hoping to get a little more mileage out of his compliment.

So, Jay didn't rush up to the boss when he was surrounded by well-wishers. Instead, he waited until the next day. He sought out the boss and commented, "I've been thinking about what you said about improving company operations. It seems to me we could implement your idea in the orders department if we ...."

Both were pleased. The boss received a well-deserved compliment, and he noticed Jay just the way Jay had hoped he would.

- **Respond slowly.** Take a minute after the speaker has stopped speaking to gather your thoughts before you speak—this is the ultimate compliment.

Flattery

Flattery is an important aspect of speech. Knowing when and how to use it is especially helpful at work. You'll want to use it to motivate people, but not to the point that your coworkers begin to find you overattentive.

There are three basic rules to giving good flattery:

- **Keep it honest.** Dishonest flattery is always suspect and often unwelcome.
- **Keep it relevant.** It is not your place to praise your superior on how he or she is handling a personal dilemma (e.g., a nasty divorce). Flattery in the workplace should be related to work performance.
- **Keep it straightforward.** Gushing always sounds insincere, even when it isn't. Yes, you *can* overdo it, and yes, it sounds bad.

 Question & Answer

Q: I manage a team of three people. I'm a very direct person—blunt even—and I fear that I'm not very good at critiquing the work of others. Any hints?

A: Make a point of pairing every critical comment with a positive one. This strategy will stretch out what you say as well as soften it. Also helpful is something called the sandwich approach. Sandwich the negative comment between two positive ones, even the same positive one mentioned twice.

Humor

Humor is a very tricky thing to use at work, especially these days when so many people are so easily offended. Because humor can easily backfire, it's better not to become known as the office joker or cutup, at least not if you want to be considered management material.

Humor often reveals your prejudices, purposefully or inadvertently. Never tell a joke you know or suspect might be offensive to any possible listeners, and then insist that you were only joking. This kind of behavior is inexcusable. If you suspect that a joke might be construed as politically incorrect, it probably is—and you probably shouldn't tell it.

On the other hand, office life is occasionally lightened by a good or well-told joke, and good storytelling is a time-honored route to popularity.

Some subjects are never appropriate to joke about. These include

- religion,
- race or ethnicity,
- sex,
- sexual preference,
- physical appearance, and
- handicaps of any kind.

SPEECHES AND DEMONSTRATIONS

If you learn to speak well, you will sometimes be asked to represent the company by giving a presentation—a speech or a demonstration. Even a practiced speaker can find this prospect a little scary, but it won't be if you know what to do.

First of all, find out what's expected of you:

- How long should you speak?
- Are visual aids expected?
- Who will be your audience?
- How large will the audience be?

All this information will help you craft your presentation.

Next, prepare your presentation. Only very few people can stand up and speak extemporaneously; you should not count on being one of these persons. Read a few good books on speech-giving if you've never done it before. Then, research what you want to say.

Write your speech, then memorize it. It's okay to use note cards, but the best speeches are still the ones that the speaker knows cold. The cards should only be there in case you block and can't remember anything.

Finally, practice your speech, preferably in front of someone else. There are two reasons to do this. One is to time your speech to be sure it is an acceptable length. The other is to have someone critique it before you give it so you can revise it if necessary.

If you prepare a speech this way, there's little chance that you won't be successful.

Guidelines: Improving Your Speech

Here are three ways to make your speech even more interesting and powerful:

- **Use statistics.** "Thirty percent of working women" is a stronger phrase than "Many women."
- **Use facts.** Do the research; then you can say, "Surveys show that ...."
- **Use concrete examples.** Tall about "Sally, a divorced mother of two" rather than "many divorced mothers."

And Remember ...

- A pleasant speaking voice is one key to advancement.
- You can learn to speak well.
- Listening is half of what it takes to be a good conversationalist.
- It's up to you to decide whether to use a dialect, jargon, or other special modes of speech.
- When wisely used, flattery and humor have an important role to play in office life, but both are best used sparingly.

CHAPTER 14

NEGOTIATING IN THE OFFICE

As is true of much of life, just about everything in office life requires some degree of negotiation. Having this skill makes you a valued employee. Even when you're asking for a raise, your boss will respect your ability to reason and compromise.

All negotiation is about give and take. In a successful negotiation, you don't get everything you ask for or want, and neither does the other side. Still, each side feels as if it has "won" something. This exercise is called win-win negotiation. If you plan your negotiations so that everyone wins a little bit, even if they have to give up something, you will have much happier—and far more successful—negotiations.

ASKING FOR A RAISE

From your view, asking for a raise is one of the most important negotiations you ever undertake at work. Many employees, especially young or inexperienced ones, believe that the boss will simply take care of them and that they need not ask for a raise.

However, this situation is true only in very large companies, where annual reviews and raises are automatic. Even so, the savvy employee knows that it is possible—and occasionally necessary—to break ranks and strike a unique deal.

As for the idea that the boss will take care of you, this is a passive posture that is typical of low-echelon employees. One way to break out and get noticed by the boss is to negotiate for a raise.

Here are some hints on doing this:

- **Earn the boss's respect first.** Work hard, and do a good job. Have something to flaunt.
- **Make your case.** Never ask for a raise without doing your homework first. Review what you have accomplished since your last raise or review. Preferably, have hard facts and statistics to back this up. Rehearse what you're going to say.
- **Prepare a rebuttal.** Many bosses explain why they can't give raises. Be sure you have well-prepared responses to your boss's reasons.
- **Determine what you want—then ask for more.** Are you hoping for a 10 percent raise? Then ask for 25 percent. Are you interested in a leased car that the company pays for? Then ask for that—and a life insurance policy. The idea is that in the compromise, you'll get at least what you really want.
- **Choose your moment.** There are good and bad times to ask for a raise. The best time is when you have just accomplished something—a project or an important report, for example. Some experts suggest asking when you return from vacation, when your boss is likely to have missed you.
- **Show off your results.** Begin by describing what you have accomplished since your last raise or review. Point out that you have successfully surveyed your customers' reordering habits and have prepared a report, or that you have presided over the reorganization of your department and were on the team to examine new products. If sales are up, by all means emphasize it. Even if your boss knows all this, take a minute or two to review the facts, because doing so sets the stage for your request.
- **Talk about you, not your boss.** This is about what you need and want, not what your boss has or hasn't done. Your attitude should be, "I've done a good job for you, and I'd like to be rewarded." Your boss may not respond favorably to, "You've let me down and haven't given me a raise as promised."
- **Suggest a solution or a compromise.** This tactic is really seizing the bull by the horns. If your boss offers a 4-percent raise when you are asking for 20 percent (this is why you always should ask for more), be ready to reply,

"Look, can we meet more in the middle here? Say, a 10-percent raise rather than the 20 percent I was hoping to get?" The worst thing that he or she can say is "No," and the best is "Yes."

- **Leave the door open for future negotiations.** If your boss says that a raise is simply out of the question right now, prepare him or her for what is to come. Say, "Well, I'm sorry to hear that. I'm going to come right back to you in three months or when the company's future looks brighter, whichever comes first."

 ## Guidelines: When To Ask for a Raise

There are good and bad reasons to request a raise. Bosses prefer good reasons, and you are more likely to get what you want if you use them.

Good Reasons	Bad Reasons
Production is up	You're getting a divorce
Operations are smoother than before	Your rent has gone up
Your work load has increased	You have added job responsibilities
You want to buy a new car	You're a year older
You successfully completed a major project	You didn't win the lottery

---

Assertiveness Works

As difficult and scary as it can be to assert yourself with your superior, remember two things:

- **Ask.** If you don't ask, you definitely won't get.
- **Stick to your guns.** Even if you put the boss on the spot, he or she will probably admire your tenacity—and your negotiating skills.

ASKING FOR A PROMOTION

Employees rarely ask for promotions for the simple reason that most bosses like to choose who to promote and when. Sometimes it is necessary to let your boss know that you would like to be considered for advancement. You'll want or need to do this when you feel that you are the right person for the job but might be overlooked because you're young or relatively new with the company.

Guidelines: Negotiating for a Raise

Just as employees mount campaigns to get a raise, bosses also have their strategies for not giving them. Here are the three strategies most commonly used by bosses, with suggestions for how to counter them:

Strategy #1: **Not now.** Bosses often put off employees until an undetermined later date by saying, "Let's talk after the (convention, the annual meeting, the budget meeting)." You name it; bosses say it.

Counterstrategy #1: This counterstrategy takes courage, but it is occasionally worthwhile to persist. You can apologize for doing so, but don't slow down one bit. Say, "I'm sorry to be so persistent, but I'm feeling a crunch, too. I've been working really hard, and I'd feel better about doing this if I were rewarded in some way." This tactic often is an eye-opener to the boss, and that's what you need in this situation.

Strategy #2: **The pre-emptive raise.** Some bosses are masters at giving raises just before they're requested. Pre-emptive raises invariably are for less than one would ask for.

Counterstrategy #2: When the boss offers you a pre-emptive raise of, say, 4 percent, counter, "I appreciate the gesture, but my financial needs have grown, and I was going to ask you for a 20-percent increase. What do you say we compromise with an increase of 10 or 12 percent?"

Strategy #3: **Promotion, no raise.** The boss hopes you'll be grateful for the new title and overlook the fact that your compensation won't change one bit.

Counterstrategy #3: Apologize and turn down the promotion. Say, "Sorry, but I'd really want to do the job right. I'm afraid I'd need a raise proportional to the increased responsibility." Alternately, you can accept the promotion on the condition that you will be given a hefty raise in a few months, after you have had a chance to prove yourself.

Prepare your promotion pitch much as you would prepare to ask for a raise. Here are some hints on how to go about presenting yourself for advancement:

THE RIGHT PROTOCOL

Sharon wants a substantial raise this year, and she is planning to tell her boss she has another job offer, but she really doesn't. Is this the right thing to do?

The right protocol is for Sharon to go out and get herself another offer, which she can then use as a bargaining chip with the boss, to get the raise she wants. It's never a good idea to lie when negotiating, because the boss may call your bluff and tell you to take the other job.

Some companies will make a strong counteroffer to keep a valued employee. Usually, though, they do this only once. The second time you go to a boss with a job offer, he or she is quite likely to let you accept the other job.

DEALING WITH CUSTOMERS

Customer negotiations are mostly salesmanship. In some ways, they're also the easiest kind of negotiations. It's not that you don't have to work hard to get customers, but making the sale is usually a pleasant event—something that is not always the case with coworker negotiations.

Furthermore, you will work hard to make these win-win negotiations, so that everyone walks away feeling good about the outcome. You win a customer, who gets the price he or she wants plus some other concessions, and you both go off happily to celebrate.

Everything that works with your coworkers also applies to customers. Plus, here are a few special hints for negotiating with customers:

- **Establish rapport.** Even in America, where everything happens fast and everyone is instantly your friend, you need to establish relationships and build trust before people will be willing to do business with you. If you've built trust, your client will be more likely to believe you when you start a sales pitch.
- **Understand your customer's point of view, inside and out.** If you know exactly why your customer is reluctant to pay your price or why your customer prefers someone else's products to yours, then you know how to chip away at his or her defenses.
- **Confirm your customer's views.** Listen to them carefully, then acknowledge them. For example, you might say, "Yes, we are more expensive than our competition, but we're also the best. Let me tell you why."

- **Use positive language.** Never say, "You'll be sorry if you don't work with us." This is tantamount to a challenge. Instead, frame everything in an upbeat way: "You'll be pleased if you go with us" or "We'll be good for you."
- **When you're ready to do some serious dealing, make a change.** Invite the customer to dinner or for drinks, someplace where you can settle down and really hammer out a deal. If your customer has been coming to you, you go to him or her. And vice versa: If you've been going to your customer, invite him or her to come to you.
- **When you start serious negotiations, get less formal.** Take off your jacket and roll up your sleeves. Meet over drinks or lunch if you've been meeting only in offices.
- **Sweeten the pot when you're ready to close the deal.** Give your customer something extra that makes the deal especially appealing.
- **Let silence work for you.** Never be afraid to be quiet. It gives the other person time to think, and it gives you time to review your thoughts and make sure you haven't forgotten anything. It also signals that you have given what you are going to give, and it's time to wrap things up.
- **Close the deal.** Don't let your customer wriggle out by saying that he or she has got to think about it some more. Counter with, "Here's an idea. Why don't you try us for now, and if you don't like it, we'll make it easy for you to cancel. But let's get you started right away." Many a salesperson has let negotiations go down the tubes simply because he or she didn't say what was necessary to close the sale.

And Remember ...

- The golden rule of negotiations is to give a little so you can get a little—or a lot—back.
- Asking for a raise or a promotion is an excellent opportunity to display your negotiating skills.
- Prepare before you negotiate.
- Really listen to the other person's point of view. It's ammunition you can use later.
- Respond to strong emotions with calm ones.
- Be conciliatory, especially when the negotiations are over.

CHAPTER | 15

DIVERSITY IN THE WORKPLACE

It's a fact of office life these days. Employees display a colorful array of diversity in religion, race, ethnicity, gender, and sexual orientation—something that was not the case even 20 years ago, when the majority of workers were white family men. Conformity was much more important then than it is today.

Today, people value their differences and bring them to work. They expect the workplace to accommodate them, rather than the other way around. This change has brought a whole new set of guidelines designed to help people get along. In this chapter, you will learn how to handle the cultural differences that you will encounter on the job.

RESPECT DIFFERENCES

The single best thing you can do to ensure that you get along with everyone is to respect each and every person. Throw out any preconceived notions you might have, and learn to appreciate and enjoy differences without becoming overly focused on them. After all, as members of the human race, we share far more similarities than differences.

Focusing on Similarities

You will get along best with coworkers of all backgrounds and preferences if you never think of how someone is *unlike* you. Instead, focus on the ways that someone is *like* you and the issues and interests that you have in common.

Never refer to another person as one of "those people," "you people," or any name that might be considered derogatory.

🔍 CASE HISTORY

Ethan, a practicing Jew, took a job with a firm where few Jewish people worked—and none as religious as he. Many people at the company, including Ethan's boss, seemed to have had little contact with Jews and therefore were not familiar with Jewish customs.

Thus, Ethan chose not to draw attention to his religious beliefs or practices. When he took a day off for a religious holiday, he never announced it as such; he simply took a vacation day. Although he was privately relieved that his boss took so little note of his religion, he was also surprised to find himself feeling put out.

When Ethan's father died, he stayed home for a week but did not announce that he was observing the Jewish custom of sitting shiva, a formal period of mourning. To his surprise, his boss paid a shiva call one night after work. Deeply touched, Ethan asked his boss how he knew to do this. Both men were pleased with the boss's answer, which was that he had asked someone what he could do.

When Ethan returned to work, he didn't discuss his religious beliefs with his boss any more than he had before. However, their relationship felt less strained because Ethan understood from his boss's sensitive gesture that his religious beliefs were respected.

Ethan's boss, who had been worried about going to someone's home without an invitation, also learned something—namely, that it is sometimes helpful to push the boundary of work life a little to make a fellow worker truly comfortable with his or her work environment. Often it is not our words but our actions that most strongly reveal our lack of prejudice.

Fighting Stereotypes

When you become friends with someone whose heritage or philosophy is different than yours, forget all the stereotypes you have ever learned or heard. Most stereotypes are misleading at best, and even when they contain a bit of truth, there are always many exceptions. Learn to look at and accept people as individuals, not as members of a group.

While you do this, don't look at people as exceptions, either. Most people are proud of their heritage and beliefs, and they don't think that they got ahead because they are different from others in their group. It is no compliment to an African American, for example, for you to say that he or she is not like other African Americans. Nor will a female executive be flattered to hear that you like her because she's not like "those radical feminists" or other "aggressive women."

 Question & Answer

Q: I'm an African-American accountant. A fellow worker is driving me crazy. Every time a certain kind of popular music comes on the radio, he says that all "my people" are musical. Because I listen to only classical music, I find this a particularly offensive stereotype. I'd like to tell him off, but is there a better way?

A: Yes, there is a better way. The next time your coworker airs his prejudice—and that is what it is, even though he probably doesn't realize it—look him straight in the eye, smile, and lightly say, "That's right. All that musical talent sure got me where I am today."

Revealing Details

Be careful not to assume generalities about members of a particular ethnic group. Many people, for example, assume that all Asians are Buddhists and that all African Americans like to eat barbecued meat. The truth is that many Asians—especially those who have immigrated to the West—are Christian, and not all African Americans like barbecue.

If you want to befriend someone, then do not assume who that person is; let that person reveal who he or she is at his or her own pace. People do not share their differences with another until they have built some trust, and nothing undermines trust more than bringing a roster of untrue assumptions into a friendship.

When you are in the process of becoming friends with someone, assume nothing; believe only what you have been told or have seen with your own eyes.

Name-Calling

For hundreds of years and in most cultures, people have made up names for people they view as different from themselves, whether by reason of race, gender, religion, or sexual orientation. These names are used to express contempt and to make the name-caller feel superior, even though he or she is not. These names cause great pain and anger among the people toward whom they are directed.

Until about 30 years ago, some of these derogatory names were used in public, and even in people's places of work. Fortunately, this is no longer acceptable behavior. Against the accepted norm, some people persist in name-calling. Even if you use denigrating expressions for other people privately, it is never acceptable to use them at work, even in jest. Nor is it permissible to use a derogatory name and then insist that it is not or that you don't mean it "that way."

The flip side of this coin is that people should always be called whatever they prefer to be called—not what others think is appropriate. The best example of this is the way that the names for African Americans have evolved in our society. Before the civil-rights movement in the 1960s, people with black skin were politely called Negroes. After the civil-rights movement, they wanted to be called Blacks. The word Negro, which had been considered a polite name up to that point, took on a derogatory, degrading connotation. It is no longer acceptable for someone to use the word Negro and claim that he or she doesn't mean it in a degrading way.

Another evolution took place more recently. Blacks began to call themselves African Americans, as well as Blacks.

CURIOSITY ABOUT OTHERS

It is only natural to be curious about another person's customs, traditions, and practices. As we mingle in our social lives and at work, we naturally want to know more about one another. This curiosity is good, because the more we learn about each other, the more understanding we are.

Even though curiosity is a good thing, it isn't always polite to ask people direct questions about themselves or about the traits that set them apart from you. When you want to know more about someone, here are some suggestions for how to go about it:

- **Learn something about the culture before you ask.** This knowledge will keep you from asking simplistic or silly questions. A lot of information about other people can be gleaned by reading newspapers and magazines, watching television and listening to the radio, and simply observing people.
- **Ask carefully and politely.** Never ask, "You people like music, don't you?" even if this question is followed by something positive. It is far better to say, "What kind of music do you like?"
- **Honesty is a good and sometimes refreshing approach.** You might simply say, "I'm curious to know more about your religion (or life, or heritage)" or even, "I'd really like to know more about your culture, but I've been too shy to ask."
- **Respond positively when you learn something.** Say, "That's so interesting!" or "Fascinating!" Saying less positive things such as "That's really weird." or "How strange!" is likely to close down any line of communication you have managed to open.

Questions You Can Ask

There are some safe topics of discussion, subjects that almost all people like to talk about. These topics are okay to raise with someone whose world is different from yours, provided you do so politely. Some safe—and interesting—topics to discuss include

- eating and food,
- children,
- daily public life,
- holidays,
- origins,
- customs, and
- ceremonies.

Questions Better Not Asked

You will not be surprised to learn that there also are subjects you should not raise, no matter how well you know someone.

Americans are known for their openness in conversation and for considering almost no subject off-limits. People from other cultures are sometimes quite reticent about discussing the very things that American love to talk about (e.g., sex, politics, and money).

These topics are taboo in many cultures:

- **Sex.** Don't consider discussing it—even with married people—until you have forged a real bond of friendship, and then only when you are sure this won't prove too embarrassing for your friend.
- **Money and spending habits.** Believe it or not, in some cultures, money is a more taboo subject than sex. Assume you cannot discuss this until your friend brings up the topic.
- **Enemies.** Changes in national political structures have created waves of immigration around the world, but this doesn't mean that people want to discuss what may be a very painful subject with a stranger or the merely curious.
- **Wars, conflicts, and famines.** Watching these events on television is a far cry from living through them. Realize that these are extremely painful subjects to many of America's newest immigrants, so painful that they may not be able to discuss them at all.
- **Embarrassing political events.** If you want to be friends with someone, it's probably better not to mention the last time your country beat up on his or hers, or any other incidents in which his or her country lost face because of yours. Others tend to treat these losses far more seriously than many Americans do.
- **Hot contemporary issues.** New immigrants may well have opinions about abortion, homosexuality, and premarital sex, but they may be reluctant to express them around anyone they do not know well. They may not want to offend you.

SAVING FACE

In most of the rest of the world, the notion of "face," or pride, is a far more important concept than it is in the United States. Americans don't necessarily mind being embarrassed. In fact, they have a marvelous capacity to shrug it off and laugh at themselves.

Many people in other cultures, however, believe that one person should never cause another one to feel humiliation or shame. Entire social systems and forms of etiquette are constructed to avoid situations where this could happen. Furthermore, a situation that may not embarrass an American—a lack of spending money, or getting fired, for example—may be an extreme embarrassment to someone from another culture.

It doesn't matter whether the humiliation is intentional. People who do business in other countries often learn that entire deals can fall apart—and that they can find it impossible to conduct any further business—if they unknowingly embarrass the people with whom they are trying to work. This is how important "face" is around the world.

All in all, you will find it much easier to get along with colleagues from other cultures if you are sensitive to issues that might cause embarrassment and humiliation. Here are two general guidelines for protecting or saving face in others:

- **Never laugh at someone's mistakes.** Ignore them. If you must offer a correction, do so gently, tactfully, and privately.
- **Don't joke with others about their mistakes.** This very American practice often horrifies people from other cultures.

OFFICE ETIQUETTE ABROAD

It is important to realize that other people may have customs and practices exactly opposite our own. You must be aware of local customs when you visit someone on business in his or her own country.

For instance, in American business circles, it is customary for the most powerful person to go through a doorway first. In much of the Middle East, though, the reverse is considered polite. The host always goes through doorways first—something that an American might find offensive if he or she did not know about this custom.

In Japan, meals are served and gifts are given accompanied by excessive apologies. The host may say, "The food is not good enough" or "The present is not worthy of its recipient." These comments can make an American who does not understand the custom feel slighted. The Japanese host is not indicating that he or she doesn't care enough to serve the very best; rather, it is exactly the opposite. The host is saying that nothing is good enough for the guest, that the guest is a special friend.

Understanding these two examples—and there are many more from other cultures—makes one more aware of the need to be sensitive in the presence of people from different cultures.

THE RIGHT PROTOCOL

Some Muslims who worked for a manufacturing firm in the Midwest were offended that the company cafeteria often served pork without offering any alternate source of protein. Muhammad was selected by his fellow believers to express their discomfort to management. He didn't know whom to approach, though. He thought he should start with the company president. Was he right?

The right protocol in this situation—which, incidentally, is more common that one would imagine, given today's diverse workplace—is for Muhammad to go first to his boss, even though his boss may not be the person who can change the situation. Muhammad's boss would be offended to hear the news from his superior instead of his subordinate.

Muhammad should ask to meet with his boss to explain the complaint he and his Muslim friends have. He should say that although his boss may not be able to help them directly, he wanted to ask who he should contact about remedying the situation.

A WOMAN'S PLACE

Despite many changes in office life, a great deal of prejudice, subtle and not, is still directed at women. This prejudice doesn't often rise to the level of sexual harassment, but it doesn't make women's work lives any more comfortable, either.

Women need to devise ways of dealing with the bias they encounter at work, and people who do not approve of or like women in the workplace need to remember that it is not appropriate to make this attitude known.

Many of the suggestions that help us get along with people from other cultures also apply to our dealings with women. For example,

- **Leave the stereotypes at home.** A popular misconception is that women take more sick days than men and are more sickly than men in general. The truth is that women take fewer sick days than men and that they do every aspect of work just as well as men.
- **Don't tell sexist or anti-woman jokes.** It has become quite unacceptable to tell jokes about another person's race or religion, and the same should be true for jokes about women, because they are just as offensive. Some people who tell them are amazed that they give offense. The best strategy is to avoid this genre completely.

- **Avoid making generalized statements.** Statements such as "Women belong at home" and "Women are too emotional" are trite, clichéd, false, and offensive.

CASE HISTORY

When Emily was promoted, her coworker Allen—a man her senior in years and experience—turned against her. He was convinced that she had been promoted only because she was a woman and that the company needed more diversity in its management ranks.

Allen became a thorn in Emily's side, questioning her every move and making snide comments, even when he was in meetings with her and their clients.

Emily endured this behavior quietly for a few weeks, but eventually, she felt she had to say or do something. She knew that Allen could be transferred to another department, headed by a man, but this option felt like defeat to her. Instead, she chose to try another tactic first. She gave Allen a very big assignment that required them to work closely together.

As they worked on the project, Allen got a chance to see firsthand the skills and knowledge that had earned Emily her promotion. He also realized that she respected his knowledge and experience and would put it to good use.

Not only did Emily never had trouble with Allen again; she also managed to convert him into one of her biggest defenders.

GAYS AND LESBIANS

Homosexuals were once forced to hide their sexual orientation to keep their jobs, but today many are no longer willing to do this. Their new openness, however, does not necessarily mean their personal lives are up for discussion with strangers.

The same sensitivity that is applied to minorities and women should also be used with gays and lesbians:

- **Leave the stereotypes at home.** As with other groups, the stereotypes are usually wrong.
- **Avoid bigoted jokes and comments.** They are hurtful.
- **Don't use derogatory names.** To you, "It's only a joke," but the person you are referring to may take this tactlessness to heart.

Don't Ask

Some people have no interest in discussing their sexual orientation at work. You must accept this as a person's prerogative. Inquiries about another person's culture or religion can be flattering, but few people are flattered by prying into their sex lives.

A person's sexual orientation has no bearing on how well he or she does a job. So, if he or she chooses to keep that information private, you should respect those wishes.

DEALING WITH PREJUDICE

The dark side of Americans' ability to laugh at themselves is that they often think it's okay to laugh at others as well. Occasionally, someone uses biases as weapons to deliberately undermine fellow workers. Unfortunately, it is often necessary to deal with, rather than simply tolerate, bigots. If not, these bigots may feel free to continue and possibly escalate their antics.

Here are several approaches to dealing with outright prejudice at work:

- **If you can manage it, joke right back.** Turn the bias back on the person by telling a joke about his or her gender, race, or religion. This method works best in instances of blatant sexism. Where race or religion are involved, you can end up looking prejudiced yourself if you aren't careful, and in either instance, you run the risk of escalating the situation rather defusing it. But one well-told joke can take the wind out of the jokester's sails.
- **Show the person what you see.** Saying something like, "Gee, you really hate women, don't you?" may make a man whose comments are degrading to women realize what he's doing and stop.
- **Refuse to laugh or smile.** Hope that this silent gesture will make your point.
- **Lay down the law.** If nothing else works, go for the direct approach. Tell the person, politely yet firmly, that you find his or her jokes and comments offensive and that you would prefer that he or she refrain from saying such things in your presence.

Questions You Needn't Answer

You don't have to laugh at offensive jokes, and you don't have to answer rude or overly curious questions, either—even if they could educate someone about your race, religion, or culture.

When someone asks about something personal that you'd rather not discuss, one good strategy is that recommended for many years by advice columnist Ann Landers. Look at the other person with amazement and ask, "Why in the world would you want to know *that*?" This exclamation slows down all but the most persistent soul.

When You Offend

Many people who offend others do so deliberately because they are prejudiced. A few offend innocently or even subconsciously.

Perhaps you grew up using what is now considered a derogatory name. Even though you now realize how inappropriate it is and haven't used it in years, it pops out of your mouth one day without warning. When this happens, there is only one thing you can do: apologize. Don't explain, make excuses, or make light of it. Simply say that you are sorry.

And Remember ...

- Treat everyone the same, regardless of their religion, race, ethnicity, gender, or sexual orientation.
- Never ask personal questions out of idle curiosity.
- Ignore stereotypes; most are wrong.
- Treat people like individuals, but not like exceptions.
- Bigotry is defined by the person who experiences it. If it feels bad to him or her, it is.

CHAPTER 16

GIFT-GIVING AT THE OFFICE

Gift-giving is an important tradition in many offices. If you are new to office life, you may not understand the often elaborate protocol behind this custom. It may vary from one company to the next, or even from office to office within the same company. That's why it's important to get an idea of what is expected and what is appropriate where you work.

MONEY COLLECTION

Many offices organize collections to buy gifts for the big events in coworkers' lives, such as birthdays, marriages, births, and promotions. In addition, office collections are often taken when someone suffers a death in the family; "the office" typically sends flowers or makes a contribution to the family's chosen charity.

How It Works

Everyone contributes money to a "kitty" or a special occasion fund, which is then used to buy the gift that is needed. The advantages are that you may contribute less than if you bought an individual present, and the recipient of the gift gets a quite substantial gift. In addition, the burden is off you to buy a gift for someone whose tastes you may or may not know.

Most office collections are organized by employees, with the understood but often unspoken approval of management. In very small companies, everyone may be expected to contribute, whereas in larger companies, a collection may involve only one department or one group of workers.

Sometimes, the company maintains a kitty for special occasions—usually birthdays and promotions—but even when the company does this, workers often still take up collections for more personal occasions, such as births and marriages.

The Pros and Cons

Office collections are not totally free of controversy. They can, for example, be expensive and frequent. Managers may not blink at contributing $5 or $10, but to lower-level workers, this amount is a sizeable chunk of change out of a small paycheck.

Some people resent giving money to coworkers they do not know well or, in some instances, do not like. Office collections tend to be and should be universal, giving gifts to popular and unpopular workers alike.

THE RIGHT PROTOCOL

Sarah's best friend at work was getting married, and Sarah was in the wedding party. Because she will be buying a shower gift and a wedding present on her own—in addition to paying for her bridesmaid dress—Sarah didn't feel she could also afford to contribute to the office collection. Still, she didn't want to seem ungracious to the people who organized it. What was the right thing to do?

The right protocol is for Sarah to quietly explain her situation to the person who takes up the collection, who will surely understand and let her off the hook tactfully. Or, if Sarah is feeling truly magnanimous, she might chip a small amount—somewhat less than she might normally contribute.

If you are friendly with someone outside the workplace, you may find yourself faced with the expensive proposition of buying two gifts: one in the office collection and a personal one to give on your own.

Keeping an Even Keel

There are some things you can do to ensure that the office collection does not become a burden to anyone.

For one thing, if the collections have spun out of control—and they have a way of doing this over time—do something to get them under control again. Many people will love you for this. There is no reason to be shy about being the person who speaks up. It is safe to assume that if you can't afford $5 or $10 two or three times a month, there are others who feel the same way.

- **Talk to the person who organizes the collections.** Explain the situation. If you are reluctant to be the only person who speaks up, perhaps because you feel you are too new to the office or too young, organize an informal committee to do the talking.

- **Suggest a manageable contribution per gift.** Figure out this amount—say, $2 or $5—in advance of your meeting. Or, suggest that people be told there is no recommended amount and that each person should contribute whatever he or she wants.

- **Suggest a set monthly contribution to a revolving fund.** All gifts will then be bought from this fund. This option eliminates the need for multiple collections in one month and lets you plan exactly how much you will be giving.

- **Set a cost limit on the gifts.** In fact, make them small "token" gifts. This option will especially be popular if many workers are also friends outside work and find themselves giving two gifts for the same occasion. It also will be popular in a large office, where there are many gift-giving occasions.

- **Limit the number of participants.** Many offices, in attempts to include everyone, take up office-wide collections for groups that really are too large. People justifiably object to donating money for people they do not know personally. Therefore, suggest that office collections be taken up only within a department or among circles of coworkers. If you take this approach, though, do take care to be inclusive. It's rude and unkind for 7 people to participate in an office collection in an office of 10 people—unless those who are excluded have made it clear that they do not want to participate.

Giving—Graciously

Even if you manage to revamp the rules of the office collection, it probably will still exist. Because you should contribute if at all possible, try to do so cordially. Don't make people feel uncomfortable about asking you for money because you personally hate office collections.

? Question & Answer

Q: It is not the custom in my religion to send flowers to a funeral, yet I am asked several times a year to contribute money to buy funeral flowers for coworkers or their families. Must I do so?

A: The gracious thing to do is to contribute. If the tables were reversed, people would take up a collection to send you a basket of food. The point isn't whether this is your custom. It is a caring gesture that your coworkers will appreciate.

Not Giving—Graciously

If you cannot contribute, it is kinder to opt out of all collections than to do so selectively. Quietly explain to the person who handles the collection that you can't contribute right now but you hope to be able to do so soon. Offer to let him or her know when you can participate. That way, he or she won't feel obliged to ask you every time.

When Someone Can't Give

If you are the person who collects the money, always let someone who can't give off the hook gently. It is especially kind to ask that person to sign the card that accompanies the gift so he or she doesn't feel left out.

However, if someone opts out of contributing because she or he hates office collection or does not want to give, there is no need to ask him or her to sign the card.

SHOWERS AND PARTIES

Along with office collections usually come office parties, both official and unofficial. Although this practice varies from office to office, coworkers traditionally cel-

CASE HISTORY

Mary was a working mother with three small children who was trying to get back on her feet after a long period of unemployment. She loved the supportive office environment at her new job but was chagrined to discover that office collections were taken up all the time—or so it felt to her. There was no minimum amount, but even giving $10 a month was more than she could afford.

Mary didn't want to cry poor—partly out of pride but also because she knew there were others in the same situation (i.e., single mothers) who managed to contribute.

After she weighed the idea of suggesting that the office collection be stopped altogether, Mary settled on a more personal approach. She explained her situation to the person who took up the office collections. She said that she could not afford to give right then but would let her know—and be happy to contribute—as soon as she felt more financially secure.

On the actual gift-giving occasion, Mary cleverly began giving handwritten IOUs. She offered to do a small task such as make the coffee or walk to the copy department to deliver an order for her coworker.

ebrate birthdays, promotions, weddings, births, retirements, and departures—that is, when people leave to take another job.

Official versus Unofficial Parties

Of these events, only retirement and promotion parties are usually sanctioned by management. Few employers are willing to celebrate the departure of an employee who is moving on to another job. Some employers will pay for one monthly birthday cake (for all employees' birthdays in that month), but if individual birthdays are celebrated, coworkers have to pay out of their own pockets.

Friction over Unofficial Celebrations

Unofficial celebrations can become a source of friction between management and workers. A few employers encourage the parties, even going so far as to contribute a conference room or some of the food. Others, though, view these activities as strictly extracurricular and feel that they interfere with the work day.

If you sense that management does not approve, follow a few of these strategies for minimizing friction:

- **Hold the party outside the office.** Plan the party on your own time, too. Management's biggest gripe about unofficial parties is that they preoccupy workers and keep them from doing the jobs they are hired to do.

- **Schedule the party for after work.** This can be a more pleasant arrangement, because you all can linger longer and enjoy one another's company more if you don't have to rush back to work—or worse, risk your manager's wrath because you don't.

- **Be inclusive.** If you hold a party at work, during work hours, invite the entire group, department, or company (depending on the size of your office and the affair). Don't leave out one or two people because you don't especially like them or because they are difficult.

- **Avoid discussing a party in the office.** When you do plan a party that, although the guests are all fellow workers, is nevertheless private, try not to discuss it at work—especially in front of those who were not invited.

- **Don't be sexist.** Office parties and showers traditionally have been promoted by women and given by women for women. This made sense when the women who socialized at work were usually the all-female support staff. However, men have infiltrated these ranks, and they should be invited to these parties, too.

- **Don't be rankist, either.** When coworkers climb the corporate ladder, they are often no longer invited to the parties for lower-ranking colleagues that they happily attended before they began their climb. This division isn't necessary or kind. Think about inviting the boss, if you sense that he or she might like to join you or at least put in a brief appearance. Many offices have become less status conscious, and invitations to celebrations are welcomed by people on all levels.

BIRTHDAYS

The most popular and frequent celebrations in the workplace are birthdays. Whether or not the party is sponsored by the employer, if the celebration is held during the work day, keep it brief. This is not an occasion to take off the entire morning or afternoon. Bosses don't like it when employees linger too long. So, congratulate the birthday person, have a bite of cake, and then head back to your desk.

WEDDINGS

A wedding is a good-news event, something that everyone feels happy about and wants to be part of. There are two good ways to express good wishes when a coworker is getting married:

- **The office collection.** By joining forces, colleagues can buy a coworker a much nicer gift than they could afford individually.
- **Individual gifts.** If you are invited to the wedding, give a wedding gift of the size and shape that you would give to any other friend.

If you don't expect to be invited to the wedding but nevertheless want to express your good wishes, then it is appropriate to buy a smaller "token" present. To avoid imposing any obligation on the wedding couple to invite you to the wedding, it is especially tactful to present this gift after the wedding. (Wedding gifts can properly be given up to a year after the event.)

Good token wedding gift ideas include

- a bottle of wine or champagne;
- a kitchen utensil, such as wine bottle opener or a wine-saver kit;
- a cookbook or other book suitable to the occasion;
- a magazine subscription, especially one that is centered around the home; and
- two special champagne glasses, plates, or other items suitable for domestic use. (A whole place setting or eight wine glasses would be too much, but sending two of something keeps the gift in proportion and still expresses your happiness toward the new couple.)

The Guest List

It is difficult to figure out whom from work to invite to a wedding and reception. In addition, most couples have a limited guest list, most of which will be filled by family and friends. Thus, the decision about which coworkers to invite is a difficult one. You may be very friendly with someone at work yet not consider him or her truly part of your social circle.

Here are a few tips that can guide this tough decision:

- **Invite close friends who happen to be colleagues.** It is reasonable, however, to ask them to be discreet about discussing the invitation in front of people who are not invited.

- **You do not have to invite all because you invite some.** It should be understood that you will invite only coworkers who are close friends outside of the workplace.

- **Extend an invitation to the ceremony, if not to the reception.** If the office gives you a shower or a gift, this is standard practice. You may post one invitation on the office bulletin board. You needn't issue individual invitations except to close friends. When an invitation is posted in this general manner, most people understand that this is a gesture and do not attend.

- **Consider creating an invitation especially for the office.** If your wedding invitation, like many today, invites people to the wedding and reception on one card, then use your computer and your imagination to make something pretty—and appropriate—for your coworkers.

Question & Answer

Q: The office took up a collection to buy me a wedding gift, and 15 people contributed. I have a very limited guest list, and I can't invite all of these people to my wedding reception. On the other hand, I want to invite three of them because they're my close personal friends. What can—or should—I do?

A: Begin by taking your three friends into your confidence. Explain that they will be receiving personal invitations, mailed to them at home, and that you would prefer that they not say anything about this so as not to hurt other people's feelings. Then, post an invitation or a general announcement inviting everyone in the office to attend the ceremony.

HOLIDAYS

In many offices, the holiday season brings occasions for gift-giving. Not only do people exchange gifts with friends, but the whole question of gifts between employer and employee comes up.

Grab Bags

To keep the gift-giving from getting out of hand, many offices organize a grab bag. To fill a grab bag, each person buys a small gift that would be suitable for anyone in the office. These presents are then put into a bag and passed out at random or in some other manner.

The advantages of a grab-bag event are that everyone buys one small gift and that all the gifts are of approximately the same value. No one feels left out or put out. Another good aspect of grab bag is that most offices set a reasonable price limit on how much is spent—usually between $5 and $15.

Grab-bag gifts are meant to be small, impersonal, and amusing, if you can manage it. In some offices, the gifts are supposed to be unisex, but more often, you are told to buy a gift for a man or for a woman. Good grab-bag gift ideas include

- a funny tie;
- socks;
- a gift book;
- a notebook;
- a toy, such as a yo-yo, jacks, or a small piggy bank;
- a picture frame;
- a small gadget or figurine for one's desk; and
- a gag gift.

From Employer to Employee

Some employers give their employees holiday gifts, either in late December or at the New Year. Employers usually give similar or identical gifts to all their employees. Some bosses give by rank; that is, the support staff all gets one kind of gift, while the junior managers get another gift, and so on.

Employer-to-employee gifts, and the reverse, should always be appropriate. Anything listed earlier as grab-bag gift would be suitable.

To the Secretary or Personal Assistant

Even if the company hands out turkeys or some other gifts, many bosses will still buy a gift for a secretary or personal assistant. Such gifts can cause talk, so there is a right and a wrong way to give them, just as there are appropriate and inappropriate gifts.

The following gifts are not appropriate for this kind of gift-giving:

- **Clothing of any kind, including lingerie, hosiery or tights, or makeup.** Such gifts imply a level of intimacy that presumably does not exist and will certainly embarrass, if not anger, the recipient.
- **Anything with a suggestive or romantic title.** A book or compact disc is a nice gift, as long as it is something the recipient will like and its title is not ambiguous.
- **A bonus.** Give an assistant a bonus if you like, but do not imagine that it is a substitute for a personal gift.
- **Hand-me-downs.** It is great if you promised to give your secretary your old television because you're buying a new, larger one, but this is a hand-me-down, not a present. It's the height of tackiness to pretend otherwise.

In addition, don't show unwarranted favoritism. If you have three subordinates who work on the same level, give them gifts of equal value. On the other hand, favoritism may be acceptable, for example, if you have a personal secretary who has worked for you for 40 years. It is entirely appropriate to give your secretary a larger or more substantial present than the newer employees on your staff. Be discreet about doing this.

Finally, don't use holiday gifts to reward good workers and those who aren't so good—that's what bonuses and pay raises are for.

Secretary's Day

This holiday has taken root, and few secretaries feel kindly these days if their bosses don't make at least a token gesture toward them on Secretary's Day. The most appropriate gifts for this holiday are flowers or candy, although it may be acceptable to give something more personal, such as a scarf or gloves.

From Employee to Supervisor

Just because your boss gives you a present doesn't mean that you have to give one back. If, for example, the gift you receive from your boss is really from the company, then there is no need to give your boss a present in return. If your boss gives you a personal gift, however, then you have to decide whether to give one back. Most of the time you will want to, but you should know that this is one instance where the size and cost of your gift need not match that of the present you received.

It is understood that the boss can afford to give you a lavish gift if he or she chooses to do so, and that you may not be able to afford to reciprocate in kind. You are not obliged to. Your boss is simply thanking you for your services throughout the year.

Any gift you give your boss should be appropriate, because bosses can get embarrassed, too. This gift should be carefully chosen. Try to find something related to his or her interests: golf balls or tees for a golfer, a scarf for a female who loves to accessorize, a book that he or she has mentioned, or a compact disc of his or her favorite artist. Other suitable gifts are a new business book, a key ring, a frame, or a small desk-top item.

It is also correct and quite lovely to give the boss a homemade gift—holiday cookies or a hand-painted ornament, for example. This kind of present is suitable even when the boss has given you an elaborate or expensive gift.

RETIREMENT

Too often, retirement gifts are trite or clichéd. The best way to avoid this is to find out what the retiree is planning to do in retirement and then buy a present that suits the person. If the retiree loves to cook, for example, a great gift might be a series of cooking classes. An amateur photographer might enjoy a new piece of camera equipment.

When the company gives a large retirement present, other employees often give token ones.

THANK YOU

A present you receive in the office deserves a thank you, just like any other present. If the gift was bought from an office collection, the usual practice is to write one note, which is circulated among everyone. When you receive individual presents, though, individual thank-you notes are in order.

Holiday presents do not require a hand-written thank you note. A verbal thanks on the spot is sufficient, and another mention a few days later is especially thoughtful. Grab-bag gifts are usually given anonymously, so if it is impossible to thank the giver personally, show delight and pleasure over the gift and issue a general "Thanks to whomever gave me this great gift."

When a boss presents holiday gifts to all of his or her employees, verbal thanks on the spot are sufficient. Even if you exchange personal gifts, a verbal thanks is still appropriate. But it's nice to mention a gift you especially like more than once.

And Remember ...

- Participate in office gift-giving customs if you possibly can.
- If you cannot contribute, graciously decline, explain your reasons, and express your interest for future collections.
- If giving gifts becomes burdensome, work with others to reduce the burden on everyone.
- Make sure all gifts given in the office are appropriate for the work environment.

CHAPTER | 17

JOB HUNTING WHILE EMPLOYED

Unless you truly have found the job of your dreams, sooner or later, you will want to find another job. Most people job hunt while still employed by someone else. When you decide that it is time to move on, it is important to do so in the right way. In this chapter, you will learn how to search for a job discreetly, so you can leave behind a boss and coworkers who will miss you and who would gladly work with you again.

A GREAT RÉSUMÉ

The first step in any job search is to either brush off your old résumé or write a new one.

A résumé is a sales tool. It describes your talents and work skills in the very best possible light to prospective employers. It is always written to make you look like a talented, multi-skilled, model employee. The main goal of a résumé is impress prospective employers so much that they will want to interview you.

Every résumé is made up of the same basic sections: heading, a job objective, present and past work experience, education, and references. Apart from these headings, there are a few other categories of information you can add if they are applicable. You might, for instance, add a line indicating that you're willing to travel or to relocate for a new job. If you have military experience, you should list it, too.

The "Polite" Résumé

A résumé is intended to sell someone on the idea of hiring you. A good résumé, above all else, does not waste the reader's time. It is well written and organized logically, so that the information is easy to read. In fact, one of the purposes of a résumé is to show that you can organize your thoughts and present them clearly in writing.

A résumé should be typed and, unless very short, may be single-spaced. You may use an interesting type face, but a conservative one that doesn't attract too much attention works best. A fancy font—or anything that makes your résumé unusual—can detract attention away from your capabilities and thus may backfire on you.

It is expected that you will blow your own horn in a résumé, but do this judiciously. State what you've done in very positive terms, but don't exaggerate or embellish your accomplishments or responsibilities. Remember that the people who will interview you know what you are likely to have done on your last job. There's no point in claiming that you restructured the company or engaged in merger talks when you are only a junior bookkeeper.

Guidelines: The Proper Résumé

Including all the right information on your résumé is only half the battle. Your résumé also has to be easy to read and look good on the page. Do make sure that

- the information is well organized,
- the sections are marked with clear-cut subheads,
- there are no misspellings,
- the grammar is correct,
- the page is typed,
- all names and numbers are accurate,
- the page is neatly printed, and
- there are no handwritten changes or corrections.

Heading	**John Smythe** 2401 West Drive Monroe, Nebraska 68648 Telephone: 402-555-1212 E-mail: smythe@localacces.com
Job Objective	**Job Objective:** Mid-level buying position in mid-sized to large urban or suburban hospital that requires my special expertise in cost analysis and system controls.
Work Experience	**Work Experience** **1995–Present: Monroe County Hospital, Monroe, Nebraska. Executive Assistant to Chief of Operations.** In my present job, my primary responsibility is budgeting. I prepare monthly budget reports as well as monthly memos on cost control. I also do special analyses of unusual expenditures and prepare the annual projected and actual budgets. In each of the three years of my employment, I have effected a significant annual reduction in operations and administrative costs: 　　1995—15% 　　1996—8% 　　1997—7% 　　1998—5% (projected) **1990–1995: St. Xavier Hospital, Charleston, SC. Senior Buyer.** My area of responsibility at the time of my departure was medical supplies purchasing. I set up a bid system for suppliers and was able to achieve an across-the-board annual savings of 9% through the use of bulk purchasing. I set up the storage and control system for storing bulk supplies. I began working as a bookkeeper, and was promoted to Senior Buyer in 1993.
Education	**Education** **Michigan State University, East Lansing, Michigan.** B.S., 1990. Hospital Administration major, Accounting minor. **Charleston High School, Charleston, South Carolina:** 1982-1986.
References	References furnished on request.
Other	Will relocate. Willing to travel.

In a similar vein, never lie on a résumé. Employers today routinely check various details on a résumé, such as job title and education, often after they have hired you. It is not unusual for a new employer to call your immediate past employer right after you take a job. If your new boss discovers that you have lied on your résumé, it may be grounds for firing.

Heading

The heading of your résumé should list information about how to reach you. Give your home address, and include telephone and/or fax numbers and an e-mail address that are not at work. No mode of communication is secure at work, and if you use one, you run the risk of having your job-hunting efforts revealed prematurely.

Job Objective

This section, sometimes called a summary or capsule history, is in some ways the most important part of your résumé. Spend considerable time working on it.

The job objective sets the tone for the kind of job you want. Emphasize responsibilities and skills that you enjoy, and play down—or omit—those that you don't. Similarly, if you have a skill that is particularly desirable, say so here.

You may also use the job capsule to set your sights high—to skip a job level, for example, if you can reasonably expect to do this in your next job. If you don't aim a little higher than your present position, you may well find yourself fielding offers for jobs similar to the one you have or only slightly better.

On the other hand, it is never wise to appear too grandiose in your job objective. Hardly anyone manages to leap from junior bookkeeper to vice president of operations. It is reasonable to assume, though, that with his well-thought-out résumé, Mr. Smythe may finagle a junior management position.

Work Experience

List your previous employment in concrete terms. For each job held, prospective employers will want to know who employed you, where the company was located, what your job title was, and how long you worked there.

Also describe your areas of responsibility at each job; for this you can—and perhaps should—use a little creativity. You should never lie about what you have done, but you should make yourself look as good as you possibly can when you describe how you did your past jobs.

Education

Try to be as careful and accurate in describing your education as you were in listing your past work experiences. Begin with the most recent school you attended and progress backward. Generally, you need not list any education prior to high school.

For each entry, list the name of the school, the year you graduated, your course of study, and the degree or certificate you were awarded (if applicable). Night school and any professional courses or seminars should be listed here as well.

References

Even though it is a given that you will furnish references any time you are asked to do so, most résumés still contain a line about this anyway.

Never list the names of your references on your résumé.

Other Categories

You may also decide to add one or more additional sections to your résumé. If you have military experience, for example, this should be listed separately. List the branch of the armed forces, the dates of service, any special training you received, and the fact that you got an honorable discharge—if you did. If you got another kind of discharge, it is usually better to say nothing and then to discuss this, if it comes up, during a job interview.

Under a heading called "Other," you may want to mention such things as whether you are willing to relocate or travel for work. If you won't do either of these things, it is better to say nothing.

Salary Requirements

You should never state salary requirements on a résumé or, for that matter, in a cover letter—even though some job advertisements request this information.

Salary is something to negotiate, and it is too important and possibly too flexible to be put into writing like this. Try to discuss this topic in person. However, if you feel you must address salary requirements in order to get a response to an ad, do this in your cover letter.

THE GRACIOUS COVER LETTER

You should always send out a résumé accompanied by a cover letter. Even if you know the person to whom you are sending your résumé, and even if that person has requested that you send it, include a cover letter. At minimum, enclose a brief note to say hello and remind the person who you are and that your résumé in enclosed.

A cover letter introduces you in a more personal manner than the résumé. It also is a good place to emphasize one aspect of your job goals, show what you know about the company, or tell why you are especially interested in the job.

To write a good cover letter, you'll need to do a little homework. First, try to get the name of someone to whom you can address your résumé and cover letter, because it is more effective when it is directed at a specific individual.

Use the cover letter to show your enthusiasm for the job and the company. For example, you might say, "I'm delighted to send ABC my résumé. I'm well aware of ABC's innovative, cost-cutting efforts, an area of expertise that matches my own interests."

If you feel you must mention salary requirements, then the cover letter—not your résumé—is the place to do it. Only do this if the advertisement for the job specifically requests salary information, and even then, don't state your salary needs directly. Instead, write that you are seeking a job that pays "in the high twenties or low thirties."

Many savvy job hunters ignore requests for salary requirements in ads and wait until the interview to discuss this. If your résumé is good and your job skills are strong, you probably will get an interview anyway.

Question & Answer

Q: My boss always notices when someone wears a jacket and tie to work. He invariably stops by the person's desk and asks, half jokingly, "What's the occasion—do you have a job interview today?" Well, I do have an interview next week, and I don't know what to do.

A: If you love your present job and would really rather have a raise and a promotion more than a new job, then by all means wear that tie to work. Smile like crazy when the boss stops by to ask what you are up to. If that's not the case, just laugh it off and keep your mouth shut until a better offer comes in.

NETWORKING

As soon as you begin to look for a job, you will want to update your networking skills. Even when you are not obviously looking for a job, it is important to maintain some kind of network, lest your contacts think you only get in touch with them when you want something.

Networking means you keep in touch with and do favors for persons who in turn might be able to help you—with your present or a future job. Good sources for networking include the following:

- **Professional organizations.** Groups geared to individual professions or jobs offer many benefits in addition to networking possibilities, and they are always good to join.
- **School contacts.** Most colleges and universities will help a graduate find a job at any stage of his or her career. They do not function as employment agencies, but they often have lists of companies that employ other alumni or even direct contacts. College and university career centers are especially helpful before you graduate. They arrange to bring prospective employers to the campus and set up interviews for graduating students.
- **Friends and colleagues.** Anyone you know is potentially a source of a new job. Cast a wide net when you start job hunting. Tell everyone you know that you're looking.

Building and Using It

When you meet someone who is or could be useful to you professionally, note his or her name and place of employment in case you decide to call later. If you are actively job hunting and meet someone who works for a company you'd like to work for, write a short note to that person saying that you are job hunting, and enclose your résumé. Explain that you realize that he or she doesn't hire in your field but that you would be grateful if he or she would pass along your résumé to the appropriate person.

Even when you are not actively looking, it is important to maintain your networking contacts. You can do this with written notes and occasional telephone calls. Sometimes, you will want to be in touch with someone when you aren't asking them for help or a favor. If you see a funny cartoon or an interesting article, use it as an excuse to stay in touch and send it along to someone with whom you want to network. If someone you know is promoted or changes jobs, use the occasion as an excuse to make a phone call or write a note to offer your congratulations. When you hear of a great job opportunity that doesn't meet your needs but sounds perfect for a member of your network, let him or her know.

Keep in mind as well that networking is a matter of give and take. If you want to be able to ask people for favors when you need them, you must also be willing to return them. Be attentive to how you might help others, and do so at every possible opportunity. When it is your turn to ask a favor, you will reap the rewards.

Charming Strangers

Sometimes you will find yourself networking with a stranger, a person whose name you were given by another acquaintance. This is always a slightly tricky situation, because this person owes you nothing, so there is a right and a wrong way to go about contacting a stranger.

To make a cold call or meeting more comfortable for both of you, remember these points:

- **Respect this person's expertise.** You might say, "I'm so pleased to meet you. Melissa speaks so highly of you, and of course I'm familiar with all that you have accomplished in the past year."
- **Be considerate of this person's time.** Because this person owes you nothing, you should take up as little of his or her time as possible. When you arrange a meeting, indicate that you will only need 15 minutes.
- **Follow up if there is a reason to.** If the person asks you to send your résumé after your meeting, send it off immediately with a note thanking him or her for helping you.
- **Write a thank-you note.** Acknowledge any encounter or help you are given. President George Bush, a consummate networker and infamous note writer, understood the power of staying in touch. He was much liked for his short notes to many people on all levels of life.

REFERENCES

As soon as you officially begin to job hunt, you will need to line up some references. References are people who can vouch for your abilities, talents, and devotion as a worker. Once you have held one job, references should be people with whom you have worked. Often they are past supervisors or mentors. Rarely are personal references, such as your minister or rabbi, used in business.

Before you use someone as a reference, call or write that person to ask whether you may. Then, it is especially nice to touch base with that person again each time you give out his or her name. Among other things, you can describe the prospective employer and offer suggestions about what to say that would help you get the job.

When you do get a job, take a minute to drop notes to your references, thanking them for their help and letting them know where you have relocated.

Handling a Bad Reference

Sometimes you will have a bad reference, a former employer who, for whatever reason, is not going to say very nice or helpful things about you. Sometimes employers get angry simply because you leave them, and they refuse to give glowing references. Maybe you did not do the job that the previous employer expected, so he or she is angry about this.

Whatever the reason, less-than-perfect references must be handled with special care:

- **Avoid listing a reference who will not speak well of you.** Instead, point prospective employers toward people who will speak of you in positive terms.
- **Remind the interviewer not to contact your present boss.** If your present boss is the one who would give a bad reference, then say you need to be discreet because your employer does not know that you are looking for a new job.
- **Prepare the interviewer for a bad reference.** Acknowledge what you think will happen and explain why. You might say, for example, "My present boss may not give me a glowing reference. He's a very difficult person, and although I've done my best to get along, I haven't been able to please him. In fact, while I would have preferred not to have to mention this, he is the major reason that I'm looking for another job. The turnover in his department is very high." This kind of savvy statement puts you in a good light. It signals that there is a problem, that it is not your doing, and that you have tried to resolve it—rather than run away from it.

THE RIGHT PROTOCOL

My friend Mac is negotiating with his boss for a raise. He says if he doesn't get it, he's going to tell the boss that he is job hunting. I don't think this would be a good thing to do.

It is bad protocol to tell your present boss that you are looking for a new job when you aren't. It accomplishes nothing and can even backfire on you. If you ask for a raise and are refused, it goes without saying that you may be in the job market for real before you know it. You could get fired, or you could find your life being made pretty miserable—enough so that you'll want to quit, even if you don't have another job.

All in all, telling your present boss that you are job hunting is like issuing a threat, and that's never a good thing to do.

STILL ON THE BOSS'S TIME

It is always difficult to find the time to look for one job when you're gainfully employed at another, but it certainly is less stressful from a financial point of view. Do not let your job-hunting efforts distract you in any way from your responsibilities at your present job.

Similarly, do not use company time or supplies to job hunt. More specifically, you must be careful to follow several rules:

- **Send your résumé out on personal letterhead, never the company's.** It is entirely inappropriate to use a company letterhead to job hunt, and this tactic will work against you. People who ordinarily might have interviewed you for a job will not appreciate your lack of respect for your current employer.

- **Don't use your work e-mail address.** Company-supplied e-mail is not confidential, and it's not your private line.

- **Make calls short, sweet, and local.** It's okay to make a quick local call, but no toll or long-distance calls should show up on the boss's bill because you are job hunting.

- **Keep your reasons for time off to yourself.** If you must take time off from work to go to an interview, take a personal day and say as little as possible about what you are doing. It's better to offer no reason, if you can manage it, than to lie about your absence. However, if the only way you can take off work is to offer a reason, then do so—claim that you have a doctor's appointment or must visit your sick grandmother in the hospital.

- **Keep your job-hunting efforts low-key.** If you can manage it, tell no one you have a new job until you have had a chance to tell the boss. You boss is entitled to hear the news first, and he or she deserves to hear it from you.

CASE HISTORY

Kelly told the wrong person at work that she was job hunting, and that person told her boss. When she got called into his office, she knew she had to have a strategy that would ensure that she kept her present job at least until she found another one.

From experience, Kelly knew that her boss did not look kindly on employees who quit. They were usually shown to the door the same day they announced their departure. She also did not want to lie to her boss if she didn't have to, because she felt lies had a way of coming back to haunt a person.

Fortunately, Kelly realized that she had not gone on any job interviews in the past four weeks. Thus, she told her boss that although she had been interviewing, she no longer was. She told a small white lie, namely, that she had not solicited the two interviews she had gone on but, rather, had been called about them. She smilingly said it didn't make much sense to her not to hear what kind of job someone out there might want to offer.

This explanation satisfied her boss, who suddenly seemed to value Kelly more on hearing that other employers were interested in her. Kelly learned her lesson, too. When she picked up her job search again a few weeks later, she told absolutely no one in the office.

Telephone Know-How

It is especially tricky to deal with telephone calls about job leads when you are at work. Occasionally, though, you will have to. Here are some hints on doing this:

- **Make phone calls related to your job search from outside the office.** Take a coffee break and go use your cell phone or a public phone. Come to work a little late so you can make the call from home.
- **If a prospective employer calls you at work, say you'll call back later.** It is okay to admit that you can't talk and then establish a time after work hours

when you can. After the employer has made the initial contact, he or she will understand that any real conversation has to be put off until a more appropriate time.

- **If you can and you want to, book the interview over the phone.** You will have to speak in curt, noncommittal tones, but the prospective employer who calls you at your present place of employment understands that you cannot speak freely or enthusiastically.
- **You can cut the call short.** Just say that you cannot talk at the moment and must set a time when you can call back.

And Remember ...

- Write a "polite" résumé.
- Always send your résumé with a cover letter.
- Network as graciously as you can, and you will reap the benefits.
- Maintain discretion in the workplace while you are job hunting.
- Let the boss be the first to know when you are resigning.

CHAPTER | 18

USING AN EMPLOYMENT AGENCY

Employment agencies can be an enormously helpful resource in finding a job, especially for new or inexperienced workers. They also give you a chance to practice interviewing with professionals who aren't potential employers. They also give you training for later dealings with executive recruiters, and are an important way of networking.

MAKING CONTACT

You will probably initiate the contact with an agency rather than the other way around. Executive recruitment agencies typically make their own contacts (and thus cannot be contacted by people looking for jobs), but most other employment agencies welcome calls from job hunters.

Try to choose the best agency that is available to you. This would be an agency that works in your field or profession, or perhaps an agency known for its quality—that is, careful placement. A recommendation from someone who has had a good experience with an agency is always helpful. Even if you have a recommendation, always check out an agency's reputation before you swear your allegiance.

Getting Them To Notice You

Better than contacting an agency, of course, is to have them notice you first. There are at least three ways to make this happen, all of which are ways to get noticed.

A High Profile in Your Field

Maintaining a high profile is the best way to get noticed. How do you do this? By joining a professional group, attending meetings, and generally getting involved in the group's activities. You could even go so far as to organize a meeting or panel discussion designed to draw the attention of an employment agency.

Publicity

Getting publicity is difficult, but perhaps not as difficult as you might imagine.

Start by reporting all of your professional activities to two places: professional magazines and journals and appropriate newspapers. Professional journals and magazines cram as much industry news as they can into their pages, and it is worthwhile to let them in on what you and your company are up to—which, if you're smart about this, will be one and the same thing. Write a press release yourself if there is no public relations department at your company to handle this task for you. If there is such a department, send them reports of what you're doing.

Alternately, if you feel qualified to do so, write an article about the industry or, better yet, something about your company that is worthy of publicity. Most trade journal articles are generated by companies seeking this kind of publicity. This is a good way to learn more (as you research the article) and also get your name in print.

Company news is also announced in various kinds of newspapers—your hometown newspaper, or one that specializes in local business or your industry. These papers, along with trade journals, typically report promotions. If you are promoted, ask your company to report this to business and trade publications or report it yourself. This move is especially helpful when you know you are about to job hunt.

If you work for a large corporation, it may be possible to use an in-house newsletter or other publication to drum up some publicity for yourself. Save copies of these, because they are good to wave in front of employment agency recruiters as well as potential employers.

Whenever you do any of these things, it is a good idea to want to make the company the center of your attention, lest you look like a publicity hound. Still, make sure to mention your role in the company's success.

The goal of all this publicity is to catch the eye of a job recruiter, who you hope will then call you, or to have a clipping that you can enclose with your résumé when you send it to an employment agency.

🔍 CASE HISTORY

Two years ago, Jane had a really bad encounter with the only important employment agency in her field. She had just lost her job, and she was anxious and feeling very sorry for herself when she met with the employment recruiter. Not surprisingly, she never received any calls to go on job interviews.

Since then, Jane has become much more professional. When she decided to job hunt on her own, she realized she would first have to mount a small campaign to revive her image with the employment agency. To this end, she invited a representative of the agency, but not the one she dealt with two years earlier, to be part of a panel she organized for a professional group. She chaired the panel, which cleverly put the spotlight on both her and the agent.

A week after the meeting, Jane sent her résumé to the employment agency, directed to this person's attention. She made sure the interview went smoothly, and never mentioned her earlier problem.

The interview went more than smoothly. Jane soon found herself with a great new job, thus proving that you can indeed reinvent yourself when you try.

Recommendations

The third major way to get noticed by an employment agency is to have someone mention you to them as an up-and-comer. It will be fairly easy to arrange once you realize among your business acquaintances are a number of people who like to play "matchmaker."

Matchmakers are friends and acquaintances who will be happy to help you get ahead. Ask one of them to call an agency, mention your name, and say that you will be calling. Then the stage is set for when you call.

Approaching the Agency

Your first personal contact with a job agency will come about in one of several ways:

- **Telephone.** You'll call the agency because a friend has recommended you and a recruiter wants to talk to you right away.
- **Letter and package.** If it is not so urgent that the recruiter talk to you right away, you can send your résumé along with a cover letter. If you have managed to rustle up some clippings as a result of your publicity efforts, enclose copies of these as well. This package, if put together carefully, should speak for itself and make the recruiter want to get in touch with you.
- **Answering an ad.** Employment agencies typically run advertisements in general newspapers and/or professional publications when they have a job to fill. If you respond to one of these, you will find yourself in contact with an agency. Even if the advertised job is not right for you, this initial contact may set things in motion and get the recruiter thinking about jobs that you are qualified for.

RECRUITER RELATIONS

As you begin to work with an employment agency, it is important that you understand your relationship. For starters, recruiters do not work for *you*. Most employment agencies fill job orders for *employers*, that is, the people who will hire you. Their loyalty is to employers, then, not to people like you who happen to be looking for work.

This situation has certain consequences for you. For one thing, you will want to determine whether an agency has a real job that you could apply for and actually get. Agencies sometimes continue to advertise a job that they believe is filled, and some even advertise jobs that do not exist.

When a recruiter mentions a particular job to you, try to determine whether this opportunity is live bait or simply a fishing expedition. An agent will not name a company when he or she first mentions a job to you; however, general information about the job—its industry and location, for example—should be available. Most important, a job description that lists the duties, responsibilities, and qualifications of the position should be available as well. If the agent is vague about any or all of these important facts, you should understand that there is no real job.

First Impressions

If at all possible, try to arrange to meet with an agent before letting him or her submit your name as a job candidate. Most of the time, the job recruiter will want to lay eyes on you, too.

This meeting is your chance to impress the recruiter. Here's how to do it:

- **Dress as you would for a job interview.** You may not want to wear your interview suit, because you hope to wear it a day or two later to an interview, but take care to wear a neat, clean, professional work outfit.
- **Take a copy of your résumé.** Also bring any clippings along to the interview so the recruiter can read them. Don't bring your only copies; be prepared to leave what you bring.
- **Have your references ready.** The agency may want to check these before setting up any interviews for you.

Question & Answer

Q: I have only had one job, and now that I'm looking for a new one, I don't know who to use as references. I can't use my present boss, because he doesn't know that I'm job hunting.

A: All this situation requires is a little finesse. Round up some people who can talk about your skills and work habits—bosses from summer jobs, former teachers, and colleagues from professional organizations. These are in fact all perfectly valid job references when former bosses are in short supply. Your taking the time to round up these references shows a certain kind of ingenuity.

During job interviews, level with interviewers about your situation. Say that you have rounded up some references, and then describe them. After this, it's up to your prospective employer to call them—or not.

Sell Yourself

At this stage, the recruiter will be as interested in your social skills as in your job qualifications. In other words, you have to sell your personality and ability to get along with people in addition to your skills to do the job. When talking to the recruiter, lay out what you have accomplished. Do this pretty much the same way you would during a job interview.

In addition, be sure the recruiter understands what kind of job you want. Many job recruiters have a nasty habit of trying to fit job prospects back into the pigeonhole they are already in or into a pigeonhole that needs to be filled. Your task is to make sure this does not happen by pushing and prodding the agent gently, if necessary, to find the right job for you.

Do understand that it is not the job of your recruiter to counsel you. And remember that he or she works for someone else.

In the course of selling yourself to a job recruiter, explain any problems that carry over from past jobs. These might include, for example, that you were fired from your last job, that one of your former bosses will not be giving you a rave recommendation, or that you have a slightly dishonorable discharge from the military.

Because they must answer to their clients, job recruiters do not like surprises. It is to your benefit to make sure they encounter none when they start to make inquiries about you.

Acing Your Interview

You need to make a good impression at the agency interview, because you want them to send you out on real job interviews. Here's how to ace your meeting:

- **Relax!** Even if you got fired from your last job and you haven't had an interview in five months, try to ooze confidence. This is very impressive. In an interview, eagerness easily begins to look like anxiety, so play it low-key. Very low-key.

- **Meet in the recruiter's office.** Obviously, you can't meet in yours, and the job recruiter's office is still a controlled, limited environment, which is good for you. Unless you're talking to an executive recruiter, he or she has no reason to meet you for drinks or dinner.

- **Show off your social skills.** Stand up when the recruiter walks up to you, extend your hand, and offer a firm handshake in greeting. Get ready to leave when you see the first sign that the interview is ending. Or, look really industrious and end the interview yourself by indicating that you have to get back to work.

- **If you can't say anything nice, say nothing at all.** It is never safe to badmouth past or present employers in the presence of a job recruiter, who—if he or she is any good—knows everyone in the industry. Make it a point to act loyal, even when you are feeling anything but.

- **Talk more openly than you might with a prospective employer.** Bring up problems you have had, taking care to make yourself look good in the same way that you would in a job interview. Once you have built a rapport (and assuming you do not come off as too picky), you can explain what you don't want to do on your next job or describe the personality types you don't get along with. In fact, the recruiter will find this helpful as he or she looks for the right job for you.

- **Describe your present job responsibilities in specific and concrete terms.** The job recruiter may ask for specific examples, so be prepared to explain.

- **Be brief and to the point.** In a job interview, you will spin out and plump up your job responsibilities, but with the employment agency, you do the opposite. Be straightforward and fact-oriented. Once the job recruiter knows everything, he or she may have some suggestions for what you might play up—or down—during individual job interviews.

- **Avoid talk about salary.** Remember, the recruiter works for employers. He or she will be thrilled to tell the client that you'll take a job for $35,000 instead of the $45,000 that was budgeted for the position. During an agency interview, try to talk only about general salary ranges or your requirements for a "complete package," meaning salary and benefits rolled into one—a necessarily vague amount. Say that your salary requirements depend entirely on the job. You can add that for the right job, you might be willing to take less money, but never specify how much less.

- **Be honest.** There is no benefit to overselling yourself, because the minute that a recruiter finds out you have done this, he or she will drop you.

?? Question & Answer

Q: I'm meeting with an employment agent on a Saturday morning. How should I dress?

A: This is a sensible question. Because the last thing you want is to look overeager, you probably won't want to wear your best interview suit for this meeting. Choose a nice but deliberately casual work or weekend outfit. Khakis and a nice-looking shirt, polished shoes, a sweater or sports jacket should make you look good enough to hire.

Never wear jeans, cutoffs, grunge clothes, or sports clothing to any kind of interview.

How to Turn off a Recruiter

There are two things you can do that will make a job recruiter stop working for you immediately:

- **Lying.** The recruiter looks bad if you lie and someone else discovers it, or if the lie means you are wasting his or her time. If you got fired from a job, admit it. If you have no intention of relocating for work, admit that, too.
- **Wasting his or her time.** Job recruiters place people in jobs for a living. They have to make their jobs cost-efficient. Therefore, if you are not really ready to change jobs but are simply on a fact-finding mission, do this on your own time. If you waste the recruiter's time now, you won't be able to get an appointment when you really need his or her services.

The Recruiter's Role

You can endear yourself to employment agencies if you show an understanding of what recruiters can and cannot do for you. For example, you should expect the following:

- **They can, but probably won't, offer any coaching.** This simply isn't their job. Occasionally, you'll get a nugget of advice, and you can always ask whether something is important, but recruiters are not the people to talk to when you want to lose your local dialect or learn how to dress better.
- **They will sell you.** Recruiters will sell you well if they are professional and good at what they do and if you give them the tools to work with.
- **They offer you much-welcomed confidentiality.** They will keep your name and your job-hunting efforts under wraps in a way that you probably cannot do for yourself if you conduct your own job search. This perk is helpful in general but particularly if you happen to work in a small industry, where everyone knows everybody else.
- **They offer experience.** They know what kind of jobs you can and cannot get. Although recruiters will sometimes hold you back because they judge you to not be ready for a certain kind of promotion, they generally know what kind of experience is needed for many kinds of jobs—knowledge that a new or inexperienced worker will find very helpful.
- **They debrief you.** In other words, they can tell you why you did not get a job you sought. Employment agencies know why their clients choose not to

hire a particular individual, and often recruiters will share this with job hunters.

Guidelines: Help for Job Hunters

Employment agencies don't remake job hunters, but specialists do. Most of these people—except the outplacement counselor—charge for their services, but they can be well worth the dollars you spend.

- **Career Counselor.** Do you need help figuring out what you want to be and how to go about achieving it? A career counselor can test you, talk to you, and offer valuable advice as you sort out the next logical step or even a career move.
- **Outplacement Counselor.** If you are fired or lose your job for some other reason, such as massive layoffs, your employer will sometimes arrange and pay for you to speak to an outplacement advisor. This experience is like getting the services of a career counselor for free. Always take advantage of this opportunity.
- **Image Consultant.** If you believe your image could use a little improvement, this is the person to talk to. Make sure you explain that you want to improve your career image.
- **Speech Coach.** If your communications skills are weak or you feel that you need help with a speech problem, this can be an excellent person to talk to—literally.

When the Recruiter Shouldn't Help

One thing you won't want to let an employment agency do for you if you can help it is negotiate the terms of your employment. Executive recruiters sometimes work to bring people closer together when they are negotiating the terms of a job, but on your level, most of the time, you will do far better striking your own deal with a prospective employer.

STAYING IN TOUCH

Even if an employment agency doesn't get you a job on the first try, stay in touch. Job recruiters are good people to know. To preserve your relationship, try some of these ideas:

- **Call in.** It is perfectly acceptable to ask for a debriefing if you didn't get a job. And, of course, you'll want to call your recruiter with profuse thanks if you did get the job!
- **Send a "Remember me?" note.** Even when you're not actively job hunting, or if you are but haven't had any contact with the agency for a while, send along a revised résumé and a short note.
- **Just say "Hi."** Call to say hello and remind the agency that you're still around. Do this even if you're not actively job hunting. If you are like most people, you might consider a job change if the right opportunity came along.
- **Help them out.** The best way to endear yourself to an employment agency is to tip them off to job openings and to people like you, who are good workers.

And Remember ...

- Try to make an employment agency notice you before you make contact.
- Sell yourself to an employment recruiter as strongly as you would to a prospective employer.
- Be honest. Job recruiters can't afford to find out bad things about you once they have tossed your hat into the ring for a job. If you explain any problems up front, however, they will more than likely continue to work with you.
- Never waste a recruiter's time.
- Always remember that the employment agency works for employers, not employees—like you.

CHAPTER 19

THE JOB INTERVIEW

The job interview is all about office protocol. You have the skills to do the job, or you wouldn't have been invited for an interview. The whole point of the exercise, then, is to make sure that you have a pleasant personality that will fit in well with the other workers.

Perform well socially in a job interview, and the job is yours. Do something awkward—or worse, rude—and there is probably no way you can get the job, no matter how qualified you are.

HOW TO IMPRESS

One way to look at a job interview is to think of it as a blind date. You want to impress. You want be liked. You want to be hired for a more steady relationship.

Here are nine foolproof rules that will make you look good in any job interview:

1. Dress up

It doesn't matter that you will wear jeans or shorts once you get the job. You need to dress well for the interview, or a better-dressed candidate may come along and get the job instead. It's that simple.

Your best bet is to wear a nice suit. If this outfit strikes you as too dressy for the field you work in, then settle on something less formal—perhaps a blazer and a nice pair of trousers or a skirt. Don't wear jeans, khakis, or corduroys. These are too casual. Don't wear sneakers or sandals, for the same reason.

These days, women may wear a pantsuit or pants and an unmatched jacket, although if you are interviewing with a conservative company or you work in a conservative business, you will make a stronger impression in a dress or a suit.

Short of showing up in black tie or an evening dress, you almost can't overdress for a job interview.

2. Arrive on Time

There are no exceptions and no excuses for showing up late to a job interview. Even with a plausible reason—you were stuck behind a drawbridge for an hour, for example—you still lose a lot of points when you show up late. You should have known the drawbridge might go up and scheduled extra time in case it did.

If you think it's necessary, do a trial run to find the office so there are no hitches on the day of the interview. At minimum, ask someone how to get there and how much time to allow. Then add some extra time, just in case.

3. Stand and Shake Hands

Ignore all the rules about who is supposed to initiate the handshake. When you meet your interviewer, you have a chance to show your enthusiasm. An easy, effective way to do this is to leap to your feet and extend your hand in greeting.

Please note: Try to make this the only person you shake hands with. Don't shake hands with the receptionist or the secretary who comes out to escort you to the office for the interview; this reveals your anxiety. If you make a mistake, smile graciously and forget it immediately.

4. Relax

If there ever was a time to appear calm and in control, this is it. Try to look serene from the minute you walk in the front door, because you never know who is watching you.

The less you are carrying, the more organized you will look, so ask the receptionist if you can hang up your coat, scarf, and anything else that you won't need in the outer lobby. If you cannot, then remove your coat, fold it over your arm, and organize everything else you're carrying before you head into the interview.

The night before, you may want to empty your briefcase and pack only the papers you'll need for the interview. Or, you can look really cool and carry a plain file folder. Whatever you do, the point is to have anything you will need—a copy of your résumé, clippings, and samples of your work—at your fingertips.

If you find yourself waiting for the interview to begin, sit down and pick up a magazine or a newspaper. Don't stand around twitching, even in the reception area. The receptionist is likely to report your behavior to your interviewer.

5. Be Nice to Everyone

Staff from the janitor to the human relations officer may put in his or her two cents' worth about you, so speak politely and kindly to everyone you meet.

6. Don't Chatter

Most people talk too much when they are nervous. A job seeker never looks good talking too much. Worse, you could reveal something you don't really want to reveal about yourself, such as why you got fired from your last two jobs.

However much effort it takes, think before you speak. Make a point of answering questions briefly and precisely and then closing your mouth.

7. Show Enthusiasm

A blasé attitude may be just fine in your social life, but this attitude never goes over well in a job interview.

You can have all the skill and talent in the world, but if you slouch in your chair, avoid direct eye contact, or act as if you don't care about this job, then you definitely will not get it. Employers often give jobs to less qualified candidates who charm them with their eagerness.

Remember that you show your zeal through your body language as well as what you say. So, sit up straight, don't fidget, and look and sound alert and interested in everything the interviewer says—even if you aren't all that interested.

It is a good idea to act enthusiastic even if you may not want the job. Several things can happen during the course of the interview to make you change your mind. You might get a really good description of what the job entails and discover it appeals to you, for example. The salary might be more than you thought. There may be another job better suited to your experience in the same company. Or, a job you really wanted at another company might fall through, suddenly making this job more attractive.

> ### 🔍 CASE HISTORY
>
> Margaret was a born chatterbox. In the course of a job search, she interviewed for a lot of jobs but had received no offers—usually because she literally never let the interviewer get a word in edgewise. Finally, out of desperation, she asked a friend what she was doing wrong. The friend told her what she suspected the problem was.
>
> After some consideration, Margaret asked her friend to "rehearse" job interviewing with her. This method is called role playing, and it is an excellent way to improve and smooth your interviewing skills.
>
> At her next interview, Margaret gave only brief, carefully rehearsed answers that she and her friend had worked out. She could hear, however, that she came to an oddly abrupt stop at the end of her answers, and this made her a little nervous. But she held her ground, resisted the urge to add anything, and stopped talking as soon as she had finished saying what she had to say.
>
> Margaret thought she had blown an interview for a job she really wanted by going too far in the opposite direction, but to her surprise, she got the job.

8. Sound Intelligent

Besides sounding enthusiastic, you must sound intelligent. Show signs of having done research about the company. You should be able to describe what you're looking for in a job and, more importantly, what you can do for the company.

A good interviewer will ask whether you have any questions. If he or she doesn't, you should say, "Before I go, I've got a couple of questions." Then, show that you have done your homework.

9. Know When the Interview Is Over

When the interviewer indicates that the interview is over, get up, shake hands, and leave. Don't linger. It is better to call him or her back with questions than to stand around trying to figure out whether you want to ask anything else.

One sign that the interview is ending is when the interviewer says, "It has been nice talking to you."

PLAYING HARDBALL

A few interviewers take pride in tactics that put a job seeker on edge. They think this approach reveals character traits such as whether you can think on your feet or calmly conquer frustration.

You may well be able to do these things—but probably didn't count on having to do them during a job interview. Therefore, your best bet is to know what these strategies *could be* so you can react to them.

Whether you use the methods suggested below or devise your own strategies, remember that these interviewer ploys are meant to shake your confidence. Don't let it happen.

The Waiting Game

Some interviewers do this unintentionally, and others do this deliberately, to see how you handle the situation. The innocent interviewer will apologize, get you a cup of coffee, and ask what else might make you comfortable. The not-so-innocent interviewer wants to see whether you will lose your cool, so he or she does not do much to make your wait less stressful.

Don't let the interviewer win this round. When you're told an interview will be later than you expected, don't complain. Don't whine that you could have slept later or taken a later train. Act cheerfully compliant, even if it goes against every fiber in your body.

Settle in with some reading material or a crossword puzzle, and act as if you couldn't care less. If the interviewer apologizes (sometimes these characters don't bother), smile congenially and shrug your shoulders.

Phone Calls

Again, the interviewer may have a real crisis to handle or may simply be playing you. Either way, ignore any phone calls that your interviewer takes during your meeting. If one goes on or is obviously personal, step outside the office. You can't exactly look around, because you're not an employee, but you can talk to the secretary or ask for a cup of coffee.

There is a definite benefit to this kind of escape. Sometimes, if you talk to the secretary or simply watch people working, you can overhear something useful that will help you decide whether or not this is a good company to work for.

Tough Questions

An interviewer trying to trip you up might ask,

- Why do you want to work for this company?
- What is your most important strength?
- What you consider to be your major weakness?

These are tough questions only if you don't know they are coming and have ready answers. This is a golden opportunity to make yourself look good—if you have prepared.

If you are asked to name a weakness, consider responding, "Well, I am very tenacious. I just don't quit until I've finished a project, and I'm afraid this makes me a bit of a workaholic." This "weakness" makes you look like a sterling employee.

Talking You Out of the Job

Some perverse interviewers try to talk applicants out of a job, for whatever reason. Perhaps they sense that you won't stay long, or they feel you are overqualified. Sometimes they're testing your interest or trying to increase it.

Because you will not really know at this point whether or not you want the job, the best way to counter this offensive is reassure the interviewer, in your most pleasant voice, that you are indeed extremely interested in this job.

Hang-Tough Tricks

Sometimes the interviewer really tests your ability to handle a difficult situation. He or she may instruct you to sit where there will be the least amount of communication between the two of you. In other words, the interviewer sits behind a desk and waves you onto a faraway sofa.

Another old trick is to offer you a cigarette (although this is not very effective these days, because fewer people smoke), knowing that there is no ash tray in the room. The hope is that you will light the cigarette and then have to figure out what to do with the ashes.

Then there are the interviewers who think they are menacing. They attempt to intimidate you with raised eyebrows, intense stares, and long silences after you finish speaking.

The solution to all these tricks is polite common sense. Mention that you will feel more comfortable in another chair, and then ask if you may sit in it. An interviewer can hardly decline in the face of such pleasant assertiveness. Decline the cigarette, as you should during any interview. (You should also decline offers of food, although you may accept a beverage.) If the interviewer stares, stare back—but with a smile.

There are only two things you really need to know to get you through tough moments like these. One is that, now that you are prepared, it will be hard to fluster you. The second is that whatever response you give, give it with a smile. You want the interviewer to think you're a take-charge kind of person—a take-charge kind of person with good manners.

RED-FLAG TOPICS

Many job seekers have a topic they need to handle carefully. This is usually something embarrassing, such as an unexplained gap in your employment history, why you were fired from your first job, or that you are looking for a new job because you hate your boss. These are red-flag topics, meaning that you need to answer them with extraordinary tact if you are going to save the situation and stay in the running for the job.

The first thing you need to do is have a reasonable explanation. Second, whatever explanation you offer must be couched in positive terms. Explain that you did not work for six months because you had saved some money and wanted to volunteer to build houses for Habitat for Humanity. Explain that you got laid off because the company was cutting back, by no fault of your own. And although you may believe that your present boss is a raving maniac that no one can work with, you cannot say this. Instead, say that you don't feel challenged in your present job and are looking for a job with more responsibility.

Illegal Questions

It is illegal for an employer (or a potential employer) to ask you questions about your race, religion, gender, sexual preference, marital status, or family plans. Only those who know how to handle such inquiries expertly survive the job interview to accept the job.

Another problem with these questions is that whereas some people ask them innocently, they can also be a sign of prejudice. When this is the case, you will need to consider whether you want to work in that kind of environment.

Such questions are often asked coyly or in a somewhat backhandedly, which is good, because then you can answer them (or not) just as coyly. If an interviewer says, for example, "Well, you're a pretty young woman, you probably want to get married one of these days," you can just laugh and say thank you.

Another approach is to answer the question truthfully. You may especially want to do this if you do not suspect any real prejudice in the question. When an interviewer asks, "What kind of name is that?" tell him. Similarly, if an interviewer asks whether you plan to have children, say so—then add that you don't think this will affect your ability to be a good worker.

The last approach is to address your interviewer's concerns with diplomacy. If he or she says, for example, "No other African Americans work here," then you can answer, " Well, I've always been a trailblazer, and I don't mind being the first."

Guidelines: Tough Answers to Tough Questions

Here are some ways to respond to illegal questions if you want to play (a little) hardball. Note: You may or may not get the job if you use these strategies.

- Smile and never answer the question.
- Shrug and say, "Gee, that's an interesting question." Then don't answer it.
- Smile and comment, "Oh, my, I don't know how to answer that illegal question."
- Ask, "Why in the world do you want to know that?"

Just to test whether the question was prejudiced, you might only slightly mischievously add, "And after I settle in, I'll make it my mission to recruit more African Americans to the company."

Money

It is an interesting moment in any job interview when the subject of money comes up, and one that you will want to feel on top of, without letting the interviewer feel bad about it.

If the interviewer brings up the subject of money before he or she has offered you the job, it is a good idea to tactfully defer the whole question for the moment. You can say, "Why don't we wait until you've made a formal offer before we get into that?" There isn't any reason to discuss money before you know exactly what the job entails.

Usually, it is better if the interviewer raises the issue of money. However, once in a while, for whatever reason, an interviewer doesn't get around to it. He or she has described the job, offered it to you, and is even saying "how much you'll like working here." All the while, you are sitting there thinking about only one thing: How much am I going to be paid for this?

At this point, you must speak up. Try to do this diplomatically, though. For example, if everything is settled but the question of money, then say, "Can you give me some idea of what kind of package we're talking about?" Or "Don't we have one more thing to discuss?"

THE CALL-BACK

The subject of money usually does not come up in a first interview, because only rarely will you be offered a job during the first round of interviews. If you are invited back for a second interview—unless the interviewer specifically states another reason for seeing you—the chances are pretty good that you will be offered the job.

You should always go to a second interview prepared to do some serious negotiating. You should know what you are looking for in terms of salary and benefits, what you are likely to be offered, and how you will get more than that.

Accepting an Offer

If you do work everything out—that is, you receive an offer at a salary and benefits package that pleases you—then you can do one of two things:

- **Accept on the spot.** Express your pleasure at joining the company. State clearly say that you accept the job, ask for a letter of confirmation, and work out any other details left to be worked out. Stand up and shake hands to seal the deal.
- **Ask for time to consider it.** It is perfectly okay to want to think over an offer, or to say you need to talk to your partner about it. If you ask for time, though, be considerate and tell the interviewer exactly when you will call with an answer. And be sure to call back exactly when you say you will—if not before.

Declining an Offer

Sometimes the job you thought you wanted turns out to be not quite right or at not quite the right salary when you finally receive an offer. This major disappointment can leave you with an intense urge to throw a tantrum and ask why you have been led down a garden path to nowhere.

⬛ Guidelines: Tactful but Tough Negotiations

- **If at all possible, make the other person name a price first.** If the offer is too low, the company can always come up. But if you name too low a price, you have just sold yourself short.
- **Negotiate a low offer.** When you receive an offer that you consider too low, say pleasantly yet seriously, "Well, we're very far apart, but I'd like to work this out." Then wait for an answer and hope the interviewer asks what it will take to bring you on board.
- **Don't be shy.** Laugh, then smile. Then say, "Well, I had considerably more than that in mind." Then be quiet and let the interviewer figure it out.
- **Name your price, then close your mouth.** Don't explain why you're worth it *again*. Don't babble, "Well, if that's too much, we can talk about it." Just be quiet.

Resist the urge to overreact, and simply decline the job. You can do this in person, on the spot, or you can call the interviewer after you think over the offer.

When you say no, give a reason, but take care to couch it in acceptable terms so as not to burn any bridges. If the company knows why they could not enlist you this time, they may make a better offer the next time.

If by chance you have led the company on a merry chase of your own—let's say you were just practicing your interviewing skills or on a fact-finding mission—never let on. Always sound grateful to have been offered the job. Thank them for considering you, and ask them to keep you in mind for future jobs for which you are better suited.

FOLLOW-UP

Your course of action after the interview will depend on how the interview ends. It certainly is acceptable to ask at the end of an interview, "Well, where do we go from here?" To ask this question, though, you'll probably want to have first seen some signs of interest on the interviewer's part.

If the interviewer does not offer any hints about when the company expects to make a decision, it is perfectly acceptable to ask. If the interviewer says that he or she will call you, but you haven't heard anything by a week or so or after the date by which the said decision should have been made, do call. This shows initiative, and interviewers usually respond positively—even if they don't hire you.

Right after the interview, write a brief thank-you note to your interviewer. This decidedly suave gesture could make you look like the most polished candidate in a close race.

And Remember ...

- A primary purpose of a job interview is to show off your business social skills.
- Dress appropriately for a job interview.
- Arrive on time.
- Take control of the interview by first preparing to answer difficult questions and then by being ready with some questions of your own about the company.

CHAPTER | 20

RESIGNING FROM A JOB

F ew people realize it, but there is definitely an art to resigning graciously. Instead of burning bridges, resignation is a time to think about building them—for the future.

Resigning from a job involves a certain amount of baggage. Those who are left behind sometimes feel a little betrayed. There are questions about what you didn't like about the company, your boss, or your co-workers, and people tend to see a resignation as a rejection. A well-done resignation, though, manages to avoid most of these bad impressions.

GIVING NOTICE

The act of resigning from a job usually brings about mixed emotions. It is a both happy and slightly scary occasion. Like most people, you will probably be a little nervous about approaching your boss.

Usually, resignations are done orally and in person. If your company also needs a written statement regarding your resignation, then you can provide it afterward. Resigning only in writing could be a sign of bad relations, and a resignation is in fact a last opportunity to try to fix any troubled relationships.

Often, a boss who has been difficult becomes very pleasant after you resign. Either your boss is relieved to see you go for personal reasons, or he or she realizes that you were a good employee and decides to let you know it. In any event, sooner or later, you'll have to talk to your boss to work out your departure, so you may as well start by resigning in person.

Here are some hints to help you resign successfully:

- **Give some warning.** Don't walk in and blurt out, "I quit." Instead, sit down and then say "I have some news for you" or "I have something important to discuss with you."

- **Keep the conversation upbeat.** Don't discuss past problems except in passing. After all, there is no longer any point. If your boss says, "Well, you never liked me anyway," don't answer, "That's right, I always hated you." Instead, smile and comment, "Well, we had our moments, didn't we?" Leave it at that.

- **Mend fences if necessary.** If this person is the world's worst boss, you are never going to work for him or her again—but you will need his or her recommendation for future jobs, so you want to leave on good terms. There is no advantage to leaving any other way, in fact. If there has been too much adversity in your relationship for you to ignore this fact, the best strategy may be to acknowledge this opening. You might say, "I know we haven't always gotten along, and I'm sorry. I want you to know that I have always respected you." Frankly, it's a good idea to say this even if you don't mean it.

- **Express regret.** Act sad to be leaving, even if you're laughing inside. Find something kind and tactful to say about the company. Don't do this for the company's sake, but for yours. One of the most important things to remember when you leave a job is that, in a sense, it is always with you. You will need it for future job recommendations, for networking, and for job contacts.

How Much Is Enough?

Two to three weeks lead time is enough notice to a company when you are leaving. Most bosses dislike having an ex-employee around much longer than this.

Some companies insist that any employee who resigns leave immediately, and you must always be prepared for this when you resign. Sometimes, though, you can find out in advance whether this is likely to happen.

THE RIGHT PROTOCOL

Sandra hated her boss and was afraid of her. They had never gotten along, and for the past year, Sandra's boss had gone out of her way to make Sandra's life miserable. Sandra did get along with her boss's boss, however. So, when she found a new job, she decided she wanted to avoid what she felt would be an inevitable confrontation with her boss.

Sandra's idea was to write a letter of resignation and give one copy to her boss—and another to her boss's boss. Is this the right thing to do?

The only right protocol is for Sandra to resign directly to her boss—in person, if at all possible. Her boss has a right to know about Sandra's resignation before her own boss learns about it. In fact, it is Sandra's boss's job to tell her superior.

Only if Sandra absolutely cannot muster the courage to talk to her boss, or if she truly feels that her boss will not listen to her, should Sandra resign in writing. Even then, she should try to hand her boss the letter in person and sit down immediately with her to plan the departure.

 ## Question & Answer

Q: I know I should resign to my boss, but he is in the hospital and will be for two more weeks. I don't want to wait that long to make my announcement, but what can I do?

A: These are exceptional circumstances that may call for unusual action. You need to resign to someone at work who can arrange for your departure. In this instance, you should go to your boss's boss, who will then tell your boss. If you are close—and feel it is appropriate—you can visit your boss at the hospital and tell him personally.

PLANNING YOUR DEPARTURE

One of your boss's first—and most self-interested—reactions to your resignation may be to start worrying about who is going to do your job. You will endear yourself to him if you have already thought about this.

If possible, and without overstepping your responsibility, think about someone you could recommend to take over your job. It also helps to have some idea of how you can go about tying up lose ends on your job or, in some cases, leaving instructions and notes for whomever will take over for you.

After you resign, you probably won't have much work to do. Many people think that they will be finishing projects, and thus that they should resign weeks, if not months, in advance, but this rarely happens. Instead, all you have to do is turn your work over to someone else.

Lame-Duck Manners

Once you resign, you will undoubtedly experience something that can only be called lame-duck protocol. Whatever power you had will flow away from you—almost immediately. What doesn't flow away naturally, management will most likely take away at the earliest opportunity. They may take away projects long before you leave, thus leaving you with little or nothing to do.

If this doesn't happen, stay focused on your work and do everything you told your boss you would before you leave. If this does happen, be cordial and find some way to fill the empty days. Clean out anything personal from your files (both the computer and paper files) and get them in order for the new hire. Call old friends or read books and newspapers all day if you are truly without a thing to do.

If you are asked to leave immediately, do so in an accommodating fashion. This is simply how some companies operate. In a way, you should count yourself lucky if this happens, because it is like getting a free vacation.

TELLING YOUR COWORKERS

Once you have formally resigned to your boss, you probably will want to share the news with your fellow workers. The only reason not to is if your boss asks you to keep the news quiet.

Some people like to make a big announcement, whereas others prefer to let the news filter around slowly. Either way is fine.

More Formal Good-Byes

A warm gesture is to take your boss and/or any mentors you have had out for a farewell lunch. Especially if your new job puts you on the same level, you will want to begin to build a new, more egalitarian relationship with them. Over lunch, thank your boss graciously for all that he or she has done for you.

THE RIGHT PROTOCOL

When Maria resigned from her job as an assistant accountant, her boss asked her not to tell her coworkers right away. She honored this request for two of the three weeks she agreed to stay on the job, even though she had no idea why it was important.

With her last week approaching, though, Maria wanted people to know she was leaving. She had many friends—she had worked for the company for four years—and she felt she needed some closure as well. She wasn't about to simply vanish overnight. But she also wasn't sure what was the right thing to do.

The right protocol is for Maria to have her moment to shine before she leaves. Her coworkers may want to give a farewell party for her, and she'll want to say good-bye and thank them.

Maria should start by finding out why her boss was so secretive. He probably only wanted her to keep the news quiet for a week or two. Occasionally, a boss doesn't want other employees to know someone is leaving.

In this instance, Maria should tell her boss how uncomfortable this secrecy makes her and let him know that she will tell people a few days before she leaves.

If yours is an office that gives going-away parties, you probably will receive one. In addition, it is a nice gesture on your part to bring in doughnuts or rolls one morning during your last few days.

FAREWELL PARTY

You may be lucky enough to be guest of honor at your own farewell party. This party is planned for you, and your main job is mostly to enjoy it. Here are a few hints, though, to help you in your role as guest of honor.

- **Continue to be gracious.** Maintain your stance to the very end that this has been a pleasant place to work.
- **Plan a short farewell speech.** Thank everyone who has helped you, from your superiors to the guy who works in the mailroom.
- **Consider sharing the good feeling with your family.** If your fellow workers have never met your child or your partner, now is a good time to trot them out for a guest appearance.

- **Leave at a reasonable hour.** Most people wait for the guest of honor to leave a party. Although you shouldn't eat and run, you also should be aware that some people will not leave until you do. It's a courtesy not to stay until the wee hours.

YOUR LAST DAY

If the farewell party is held before your last day of work, when you actually leave the office for the last time, try to say good-bye to everyone.

Better still, write brief thank-you notes letting people know how much you have enjoyed working for and with them. A note to a boss or a mentor should be personal, but you can write one note to be shared among your colleagues. These notes can be typed or handwritten.

And Remember ...

- Never resign until the details are worked out for your new job, with all terms and your starting date carefully planned.
- Resign to your immediate superior—in person, if at all possible.
- Do everything you can to mend fences with persons who aren't your favorites, especially if they could ever be of any help to you in the future.
- Never badmouth an employer after you resign. Smooth over any bad feelings, and try to leave on the best possible terms.

APPENDIX

ADDITIONAL RESOURCES

General Etiquette & Protocol

To learn which fork to use and how to signal the waiter that you are done eating without saying a word, you will want to spend some time with a general etiquette book.

Executive Etiquette in the New Workplace. Faux, Marian and Marjabelle Young Stewart. New York: St. Martin's Press, 1996. A useful no-nonsense guide for executives who have arrived and those who aspire to do so.

Everyday Etiquette: A Guide to Modern Manners. Fox, Grace. New York: Berkley, 1998. An easy-to-read guide to social behavior, with a special chapter on office life.

The New Etiquette: Real Manners for Real People in Real Situations. Stewart, Marjabelle Young. New York: St. Martin's Press, 1996. An etiquette encyclopedia that makes looking up the answers to specific questions easy.

General Reading

Office Basics Made Easy. Tarbell, Shirley. New York: LearningExpress, 1997. Twenty savvy lessons introduce anyone to office life.

Dressing for Work

The Winning Image: Present Yourself with Confidence and Style for Career Success. Gray, James, Jr. New York: AMACOM, 1993. More than just how to dress, this book shows you how to radiate confidence.

110 Mistakes Working Women Make and How to Avoid Them: Dressing Smart in the '90s. Nicholson, Joanna. New York: Impact, 1994. A timely primer to dressing well at work.

Dress Casually for Success...for Men. Weber, Mark. New York: McGraw-Hill, 1996. A man's guide to using dress to get ahead.

High-Tech Manners

Rules of the Net: On-Line Operating Instructions for Human Beings. Van der Leun, Gerard, and Thomas Mandel. New York: Hyperion, 1996. Cybercourtesy explained: here is all you need to know to travel the net politely.

Bosses, Employees, and Co-workers

Coping with Difficult Bosses. Bramson, Robert M. New York: Birch Lane, 1992. Excellent advice on a touchy topic.

Difficult People: How to Deal with Impossible Clients, Bosses, and Employees. Cava, Roberta. New York: Firefly, 1997. Full of good strategies.

What to Say to Get What You Want: Strong Words for 44 Challenging Types of Bosses, Employees, Co-Workers, and Customers. Deep, Sam, and Lyle Sussman. New York: Perseus, 1992. Management experts offer strategies for the toughest situations.

How to Recognize and Reward Employees. Deeprose, Donna. New York: AMACOM, 1994. Good motivational ideas that are both interesting and inexpensive.

How to Be a Star at Work: Nine Breakthrough Strategies You Need to Succeed. Kelley, Robert E. New York: Times Books, 1998. Some ideas you may not have thought of. Kelley lays out what works—and what doesn't.

1001 Ways to Energize Employees. Nelson, Bob, and Burton Morris. New York: Workman, 1997. A book whose focus is on building morale. Full of creative, easy-to-use ideas.

Customers & Clients

How to Win Customers and Keep Them for Life. Leboeuf, Michael. New York: Berkley, 1989. Sensible action-oriented approach from a leader in the field.

Customers for Life: How to Turn That One-Time Buyer into a Lifetime Customer. Sewell, Carl, and Paul B. Brown. New York: Pocket Books, 1992. Humorous and very useful advice.

Business Travel

The Business Traveler's Survival Guide: How to Get Work Done While on the Road. Longhoff, June. New York: Aegis: 1997.

202 Tips Even the Best Business Traveler May Not Know. McGinnis, Christopher J. New York: Irwin, 1994.

Buck Peterson's Guide to Indoor Life: Hotels, Conventions, Exhibitions. Peterson, Buck, and Brian Peterson. New York: Ten Speed Press, 1992.

Business Writing & Speaking

Business Communications. Barfield, Ray E., Sylvia Titis, and George T. Friedlob. New York: Barrons, 1992.

101 Ways to Captivate a Business Audience. Gaulke, Sue. New York: AMACOM, 1992. Demystifies the whole process.

Effective Business Speaking: The Basics Made Easy. McManus, Judith. New York: LearningExpress, 1998. A simple 20-step plan for immediately improving your communication skills.

Negotiations

The Complete Idiot's Guide to Winning Through Negotiation. Ilich, John. New York: Alpha Books, 1996. An excellent beginner's guide to persuasion.

Are You Paid What You're Worth? Oaks, Suzanne, ed., and Michael F. O'Malley. New York: Broadway, 1998.

Cultural Differences

Do's and Taboos Around the World in Business. Axtell, Roger, ed. New York: John Wiley & Sons, 1993. Excellent information that makes you confident anywhere in the world.

Job Hunting

The Complete Resume Guide. Faux, Marian. New York: ARCO, 1996. Special advice for persons returning to the workplace, older workers, and first-time job seekers.

Networking for Novices: The Basics Made Easy. Shelly, Susan. New York: Learning-Express, 1998. The do's and don'ts of networking. How to build and use contacts successfully.

Job Hunting Made Easy. Sonnenblick, Carol, Michaele Basciano, and Kim Crabbe. New York: LearningExpress, 1997. Twenty easy steps to a better job.